TAX-FREE RETIREMENT

10TH ANNIVERSARY EDITION

TAX-FREE
RETIREMENT

10TH ANNIVERSARY EDITION

Patrick Kelly

ISBN: 978-0-9833-615-6-5

Printed in the USA

Nationwide Praise for Tax-Free Retirement

"I've read this book. It is a great book. It puts in writing what we've preached at Kinder Brothers for 30 years. Get this book into the hands of all your clients!"

"Patrick has the uncanny ability to take a complicated idea and make it simple and easy to understand for both the practitioner as well as the layman. This is the best book I have ever read that covers this subject so thoroughly."

"I've been in the business since 1964 and this is by far the best book regarding life insurance that I have ever seen. Great ideas written with such simplicity and clarity. I have ordered many copies for my clients and it has been enthusiastically received. Congratulations!"

"As both a CPA and Financial Advisor, I have been advising clients for years regarding the importance of tax-efficiency planning. Tax-Free Retirement is a tremendous educational tool for my clients because it provides clarity regarding tax-efficient alternatives to qualified retirement plans. Patrick, thank you for helping my clients understand the benefits of the advice I have been teaching them for years!"

"FANTASTIC BOOK! No industry jargon here – just easy to understand terms that motivate people to do something!"

"Patrick's book has taken an arcane topic like life insurance from the darkness to the light. This book has made the complex issues about life insurance into simple and understandable concepts. Simply put, this should be required reading for all practitioners in the financial services arena prior to advising people. Patrick, I thank you for giving me the light."

"Patrick's book will revolutionize how people think about tax-qualified retirement plans. Who could imagine a retirement financial-strategy book that you can't put down? Patrick has done that with his 'must read' book and illustrated so clearly the magical power of an alternative to tax-qualified plans."

"This book is awesome!!"

"WOW!!! I just finished the book and have been sitting here for the last thirty minutes or so thinking about the impact the concepts you have brought to light will have on the thousands of people you will undoubtedly touch either directly or indirectly. In my own family, this will set a new direction and way of thinking for the remainder of the accumulation phase of our planning. In the distribution phase, we will have options that would not have been considered and we will have the opportunity to touch so many with so much more. Thank you."

"Amazingly easy to read and understand. Once I started reading I could not put it down. I ordered 10 books to immediately give to my clients. Thank you for making the principles in your book easy to understand."

"Patrick's easy-to-understand way of explaining things has given my clients a greater sense of clarity and the little extra nudge needed to take positive action for their future."

"Patrick has taken concepts that are increasingly being used by progressive financial services experts and extrapolated them into a language easily understood by the masses. I can't wait to get this book into the hands of my high-income, high-net-worth clients. I believe it will have a profoundly positive impact for their futures."

"Patrick, what a great book!! Your writing is very entertaining and I love the way the anticipation builds so that I couldn't wait to get to the end of the book."

"How many books on retirement planning and financial planning are so interesting you can't put them down? This is one of the few. Patrick's book not only outlines some of the mistakes people often make with their money, but presents in a simple way an alternative to retirement planning that many people are not aware of. I know both financial professionals and their clients would benefit from the ideas presented in his book."

"Patrick's book was a REAL eye-opener. I finally have a full grasp of the incredible magnitude of the LIVING BENEFITS offered by Universal Life insurance. Much more important, though, anyone can read his book and have a clear understanding of and appreciation for the true value of Universal Life. Now, I consider it my personal responsibility to share this treasure with all my higher-income clients because I can make a difference in their lives."

"Patrick has a knack for putting money concepts into words that make sense. He clarifies strategies, so they seem achievable, and the message is effective for clients at any level in their financial planning."

"Patrick's book was incredibly clear and concise. It was an enjoyable read and I found myself nodding in agreement from beginning to end. This book has helped me spend my time with only qualified prospects who are ready to move forward."

"Loved your book! It was a quick, easy read, and very understandable."

"Patrick's ideas and concepts are both easy to understand and easy to use. This is a very quick read with an abundance of practical tools to benefit any individual in their financial planning."

"Patrick's down to earth practical insights will enlighten you to make changes in your retirement planning strategies. The outcome will maximize your standard of living in your golden years, while protecting the ones you love most!"

"Outliving one's money is the number one fear of the senior community. Your book supplies the answers on how to stretch those dollars to the max. Thank you for showing us how we can help others live a more secure and better life."

"Wow! What a smooth, easy read. I felt like I was reading my own words. Your metaphors and stories are right on, accurate, and to the point. When you publish this, I'll take 50 copies."

"LOVE your book. It was like a bowl of M&M's®. Once I started I couldn't stop until I had eaten the whole bowl."

"Patrick's book is a very easy read. My copies are now in the hands of my team and my clients. The concept is easy to understand and very practical. Thank you!"

"Your book is wonderful! I have my husband reading it next."

To my family - You are God's greatest blessing.

TABLE OF CONTENTS

PART V: INDIVIDUAL APPLICATIONS

PART VI: THE NEXT STEP

Preface

Ten years ago, when I wrote the preface for my first book *Tax-Free Retirement*™, I said I hoped it would transform the lives of countless individuals around the globe. It was a dream. A hope. A grand desire. And typically I've found big dreams usually play better in the mind than in reality.

This book, however, stood that theory on its head. What has transpired over the last 10 years has been nothing short of miraculous. It's been a constant series of surprises. The people met. The places traveled. The lives changed. The stories told. And what drove all of this were simply the truths this book contained. Truths that for the first time were understandable by the masses and helped them fully comprehend a powerful accumulation strategy that has been around for decades yet still remains misunderstood and underutilized. The first edition of this book opened that door of truth to hundreds of thousands of individuals. To all of you who read that edition and passed it along to others, "Thank you." I am deeply grateful. Your support humbles me.

About twelve months ago I decided to pick this book up and read it again with fresh eyes to see if the truths I penned over a decade ago still rang with equal clarity and significance. They did. Remarkably so. In a decade that saw sweeping financial change, largely facilitated by a global credit meltdown, I found the principles in *Tax-Free Retirement*™ as fresh and salient as they were 10 years previous – maybe even more so. With that discovery I decided it was time for a refresh. Time to reawaken these perennial truths to a new generation. I also realized, with unintentional coincidence, that 2017 marked the ten-year anniversary of this book's first edition. So with the convergence of these thoughts and realizations, I present to you an updated and revised *10-year Anniversary Edition* of the book that started it all – *Tax-Free Retirement*™.

One last and very important note to every reader. While each chapter in this book carries unique truths that can be digested in isolation from the other chapters, *the book is intended to be read as a whole.* This is critical! To fully grasp the complete veracity of this strategy, you cannot skip over any chapter – each one is important and feeds the whole. The fullness of its integrity resides in the book's entirety. So please don't single out just one or two chapters and call it good. Dig deeper. Take it all in. Then and only then will you be able to decide whether this strategy is a proper and suitable fit for your specific and unique circumstances.

PART I: THE FOUNDATION

Chapter 1

A Stunning 10 Years

Sometimes all you can do is look back in wonderment and ask, "What just happened?" And from a financial standpoint the last 10 years have certainly been one of those periods in history.

When I published the first edition of *Tax-Free Retirement*™ in April of 2007, the markets were soaring and business was booming – especially the business of credit. Banks and lending institutions couldn't give money away fast enough. It was as if money was free for the asking. But then came the autumn of 2008. A chink in the armor. A crack in the dam. What began as a drip soon turned into a rushing torrent and eventually culminated in a tsunami of epic and historic proportions, unlike anything the global economy has ever seen. Even though global stock markets cratered, in many cases erasing 15 (or more) years of gains, and centuries-old banks and brokerage companies disappeared overnight, it could have been worse – a lot worse – and it almost was. By nearly all accounts the entire global economy was a gnat's-breath away from total collapse.

And though the economy avoided a final knockout punch, many individuals did not. They were hurt badly. Stunned and hanging on the ropes, their life savings pummeled to the point of non-recognition. Figuratively speaking, many 401(k)s became 201(k)s and some even 101(k)s. In other words many individuals experienced catastrophic losses that forced them to delay or even abandon their desired retirements. Their life savings had evaporated and so had their golden-year dreams.

Hindsight, however, is a beautiful thing. It gives us perspective we don't have in the moment, enabling us to look back and see what we *should* have done to protect ourselves. Unfortunately, we are not soothsayers. We can't predict the future. But what if, somehow, we *had* been able to see that disaster coming? What might we have done? Would we have sold our equities at the peak of the market on October 9, 2007, just before the stock market's precipitous decline and then bought them back on March 9, 2009, the day the markets hit their lows, riding it back up during one of the longest and uninterrupted bull markets the world has ever seen?

What could that have looked like?

But no one knew then what we know now. Hindsight is indeed 20/20. These questions are largely rhetorical in nature since all of this is now solidly in the rearview mirror. Why do I even bother to ask them? Is it to rub in your face the mistakes of your past? Is it to make you feel badly? Certainly not on both accounts. It is simply because history has a way of repeating itself. And if we allow ourselves to learn from our past misfortunes, it might help us avoid the next disaster.

And unfortunately, that pending disaster might be sooner than we think. It's possible that right now we're at a critical time to stand up, take note, and batten down our financial hatches in order to prepare for a mammoth tidal wave that has been steadily building on the horizon. A wave of incomparable proportions. A wave visible to everyone, at least everyone willing to look. A wave I've been talking about since 2010. And that wave is the debt crisis facing our nation, as well as virtually every other developed nation around the globe.

In my first edition of *Tax-Free Retirement*™, I wrote on page 85 that our national debt was over $8,500,000,000,000 (eight and a half trillion) in October of 2006. I also said it was growing at a rate of $1.6 billion per day, and in order to pay it off, each one of the 300 million Americans alive at that time would have had to contribute $28,511. That meant every man, woman, and child alive in our nation, not just every American taxpayer. And on page 86 I wrote, *"Let me put this into its overwhelming perspective. Back in 1791, yes 215 years ago, our national debt stood at $75,463,476 – a little above seventy-five million dollars. However, forty-four years later, in 1835, our national debt had been reduced to a mere $33,733. Essentially, we were nearly debt-free as a nation. From this date forward our debt has been on a steady and atmospheric rise. So in a period of 168 years (1835-2003), we managed to amass $7 trillion in debt. The extra $1.5 trillion we have tacked on in the last three years [2003-2006] represents a whopping 17% of the total debt it has taken us 171 years to accumulate. Think about that for a moment. Seventeen percent of our total national debt has occurred in the last three years or approximately 1% of the total time involved incurring this debt. Are things speeding up? Absolutely! Do you think this will slow down? No way!"[i]*

And boy was I correct – unfortunately. Since October 2006 our debt has grown, by an *additional* 133%, to the staggering sum of $19,850,000,000,000. And while the years 2003 to 2006 accounted for 17% of our total national debt at that time (or 7.5% of today's number), the last 10 years [2006-2016] have now accounted for 57% of our country's total debt accumulated since 1835.

But as I mention in my 2011 book *The Retirement Miracle*™, and as you can confirm on the websites *truthinaccounting.org* and *usdebtclock.org*, the statistics I am using are only the *published* national debt. The *real* level of our unfunded liabilities, according to these two informative sites, sits somewhere between $102 trillion and $128 trillion, more than 500% *worse* than what we are led to believe.

And while the purpose of this chapter is not to diagnose how or why we've accumulated this debt or how to fix it (though I will talk more about our nation's debt in Chapter 13), the purpose is to wake you up to the bleak situation facing America and the rest of the developed world and to point out that there is indeed a tidal wave of consequences headed our way at an ever increasing speed.

And what is this potential consequence? Higher taxation. Lots and lots of potential taxation. Why? Because bills need to be paid. It's no different than a household or a business. If bills are rapidly increasing, then the household income or the business revenue better increase just as quickly. If it doesn't, there is only one eventual outcome – bankruptcy. Debt can't keep growing forever.

This is also true with nations. But nations have an easy out, an ace up their sleeve. It's easy for them to increase their revenue, and they don't have to work a single hour longer or an ounce harder to do so. All it takes is a few hundred votes and the stroke of a pen. And voila. Presto. The bills get paid. How? You know the answer. It's the one that stares you squarely in the face every April 15th – taxes. Your hard earned income is the answer. It's the easy solution and the source of income for kings and presidents to run their nations.

Let me ask you this. If you knew with certainty (though we don't) that taxes in the future were going to be higher than they are today, what would you do? Would you pay those taxes today or wait until later, once the tax rates increased? That's an easy answer. Obviously, it would be better to pay your taxes today at a lower rate than to worry about what future tax rates might rise to. But that's not what most people are doing. The vast majority of individuals saving for retirement are packing full their tax-qualified accounts – IRAs, 401(k)s, SEPs, SIMPLEs – erroneously thinking they are saving on taxes, when in reality, all they are doing is *delaying* taxes and in doing so making them far, far, FAR worse.

When was the last time delaying a fix for any problem was the correct solution? For instance if you came home from work tonight and found a broken pipe flooding your house, what would you do? Would you call the plumber that evening, or would you wait a few weeks (or years) to have him come out and fix it? Of course, you'd fix it today. Why? Because every hour and day you waited would only create a bigger and more costly problem. In my experience problems delayed are problems magnified.

The leaky pipe scenario is so obvious it may sound silly to even ask the question; however, people are making that same mistake, each and every day, with their retirement savings. Instead of fixing the problem today (paying their taxes) they are choosing to delay it, and that delay may cost them tens or even hundreds of thousands of dollars in *additional* taxes in the future.

If you believe, as I do, that future taxation will be higher than today's, then just like calling the plumber immediately, it might be better for you to pay your taxes today, at a potentially lower rate, than to worry about paying them at a potentially higher rate in the future.

And that is why I originally wrote this book. It is also why I wanted to update it and introduce it to a new generation of savers. I wanted to show them how it is indeed possible (based on today's tax laws) to pay their taxes today, at a potentially lower tax rate, and then be able to access their savings at a later date, both principal and gain, without having to pay a single penny in tax. That's right. Zero. And that's why I named this book *Tax-Free Retirement*™.

So pull up a chair. Pour yourself some coffee. And enjoy what's waiting because you deserve it. And unlike the last financial tsunami that snuck up on all of us in 2008, if we prepare properly, we might just find ourselves out surfing the crest of this tidal wave, having the time of our lives, instead of feeling its crippling weight as it crashes on the unprepared.

Chapter 2

Why is Everybody in Such a Financial Mess?

Have I gotten your attention? I hope so because your financial future depends on it. But before we dive in and explore why the government is the eventual winner for those who fund a tax-qualified retirement plan, I need to lay some additional groundwork. You know the saying, "You can lead a horse to water, but you can't make him drink." While that may be true in a literal sense, I believe it *is* possible to get a horse to drink. All you have to do is make him thirsty. And how can you make him thirsty? Take him out for a run. Give him a salt lick. Or any number of other options. So while you can't *make* him drink, you can make him thirsty, so he *wants* to drink.

And that's what the first 16 chapters of this book are intended to do. To expose what's really going on in the world, so you'll be thirsty. Thirsty to make wise choices. Thirsty to do things differently. Thirsty to turn over a new leaf in managing your finances. And thirsty to create a plan that works for your personal situation and then stick to that plan for the long-haul.

I could lay before you a plan that makes all the sense in the world. I could show you how to avoid tax on your savings. I could razzle-dazzle you with all sorts of new information. But as good as those things are, you must know that your financial success will not be accomplished by your *knowledge* of those things. Your financial success depends solely on *your actions*. You must be thirsty enough to want to drink.

Ten years ago, when I wrote *Tax-Free Retirement*™, I said that in my 15 years in this business, I had discovered nine amazingly common financial problems that we all face. Problems I saw in such unanimity that I named them *Financial Landmines*™. Problems that everyone I had ever met with struggled with in some form or another.

I can tell you today, ten years later, that nothing has changed. These same nine problems still plague individuals – all individuals – with the same ferocity they did in 2007, and I'm certain they will continue to do so in 2027 as well. And since these *Financial Landmines*™ are common to us all, and hinder us from making good financial choices, it is critical to address each of these before we move to a solution; otherwise, it would be no better than leading a horse to water who wasn't thirsty.

Please understand this first section is a critical part of the book for everyone, even for those of you who are managing your money successfully. Trust me, there will come a day when one of these landmines will knock on your door so loudly or appear so lovely that you won't be able to deny its call. I want more for you than that. I am confident that if you avoid these nine common *Financial Landmines*™ you will find financial success few have experienced.

Then, and only then, will you be fully prepared to take advantage of all the insights of the *Tax-Free Retirement*™ strategy.

And if you avoid the *Financial Landmines*™ *and* implement the *Tax-Free Retirement*™ strategy, you could find yourself in a position to revolutionize not only your financial future but, quite literally, the future of your family, your community, and very possibly the world. Although those seem like quintessential overstatements, you will see how true they are once you conclude the last chapter of this book. So let's see if we can conjure up a good ol' fashioned thirst and prepare for a long, refreshing drink from a cold mountain stream.

PART II: AVOIDING THE
9 *FINANCIAL LANDMINES*™

Chapter 3

Landmine 1 – Lack of Planning

How is it that hundreds of thousands of Americans each year find themselves at retirement age without the necessary funds to be able to retire? What happened? Who's at fault? Is the government to blame?

Many people go to school, get a job, work forty years, retire temporarily, but find they can't afford to live; so at age 65 (or older) they go back to work at McDonald's and die during the lunch rush with a spatula in one hand and a sesame seed bun in the other. Okay, maybe it happens a little differently than that, but without the proper planning you too may find yourself setting a new Guinness World Record as the oldest person ever to assemble the "two all-beef patties, special sauce, lettuce, cheese, pickles, onions, on a sesame seed bun."

Few people ever stop long enough during the hustle of everyday life to ask some important questions: *How much money will I need to retire? At what age do I want to retire? And how will the money get there?*

Don't make that mistake.

It's easy to throw around numbers like a million dollars, but most people have no idea how much they would need to save every month to build a bank account consisting of one million dollars. Let me ask you, right now, at 5% interest how much would you have to save starting today to have one million dollars at age 65? What if the interest rate were 3% or 7%? You don't know? Why not? You see, the number one obstacle to effective saving is exactly this: people don't have a plan.

I'd be willing to bet there isn't one out of 10,000 people who could answer that question without sitting down with a financial calculator to figure it out. It seems our society trains us *not* to know or to care. We are called to spend, spend, spend and, once the money is gone, to pull out the plastic and spend some more.

Most people give their attention and effort to how much they are going to spend, not to how much they are going to save. Or if they do save, their only plan is to sock away whatever is left over after all the bills are paid. The obvious problem? There is usually nothing left over – regardless of whether the person is making $30,000 or $300,000. Without a plan it usually *all* gets spent.

Saving money has almost become un-American. In their best-selling book *Your Money or Your Life*, Joe Dominguez and Vicki Rubin report, "The savings rate (savings as a percent of disposable income) was 4.5% in 1990 (and was as low as 4.1 percent in 1988), whereas in 1973 Americans saved an average of 8.6 percent. The Japanese, by the way, save over 15 percent of their disposable income."[ii]

What's wrong with this picture? Most Americans don't have a plan. Remember, as the old adage says, *People don't plan to fail; they fail to plan.* As I look at the above statistics, it is evident to me that we are a nation of individuals who have lost the art of saving. We see a toy and we buy it. We drive by a bigger house and we get it. We envy our neighbor's car so we duplicate (or surpass) it.

Maybe you find yourself losing the savings battle because you don't have a plan. What can you do? The answer is easy – build one. Let me walk you through the practical steps necessary to build and *implement* (that is the key) a practical and workable savings plan.

Step 1: Set a Goal

Decide how much money you need (or want) to accumulate and how many years you have to reach that goal. For instance, if you are currently 35 years old and want to build a nest egg of $1,500,000 by the time you reach 65 (which by the way would only be worth $610,540 in today's dollars with a modest 3% inflation), how much would you need to save each month? I think you'll be shocked by the answer.

Monthly contribution necessary for a 35 year old to save $1,500,000 by age 65

Interest Rate Monthly	Contribution Necessary
3%	$2,567.64
5%	$1,794.85
7%	$1,222.41

Figure 3.1

The only variable in this chart is the interest rate. The length of time for each example is exactly the same. I told you the results would be shocking. Albert Einstein once said, "Compound interest is the eighth wonder of the world. He who understands it, earns it ... he who doesn't ... pays it."[iii] Based on these figures, I'm sure you'd agree.

As a little child, I remember my mom asking me an interesting question. Maybe you've been asked the same one. She was using this question as a teaching tool in regards to the amazing power of compound interest. It was obviously a good one because it has stayed with me throughout the years.

"Patrick," she said, "Would you rather have someone give you $1,000,000 or a penny that doubled its value every day for a month?"

"A million dollars for sure!" I replied. That was when a million dollars was all the money in the world. I was sure it would take a thousand years of doubling for that penny to be worth a whole million dollars.

She looked at me with a smile and said, "I want you to go and figure out how much that penny would be worth after a month of doubling every day and then come back and tell me which one you would rather have."

"Okay," I said. Then I was off to begin my manual calculations.

It was a good exercise to work through manually to see when that penny really began to grow in value, but I'll save you the steps and amaze you with the answer. That penny is worth almost *eleven times* that million-dollar offer for a 30-day month ($10,737,418.24 to be exact) and *twenty-one and a half times* more than the million-dollar offer for a 31-day month ($21,474,836.48 to be precise).

Now, which would you rather have?

Are you beginning to see the incredible power of compound interest?

Step 2: Pay Yourself First

Now that you have the makings for an effective roadmap for your future investment goals, how are you actually going to find the money in your budget to put away for the future? If you're like most people, you realize that most of the time there is more month than money.

So if you are maxed out right now, you may be wondering where the money is going to come from to fulfill your newly designed plan? The answer is a very simple principle that any financial planner worth their salt would espouse, yet a plan that very few people actually practice. It is this: Pay yourself first.

Who is the first person to take money from your monthly income? Uncle Sam of course. He never misses. No matter how much or how little you make, he always gets his cut. Why? He gets paid first. There is always money for him to take. How well would it work if Uncle Sam said, "Go ahead and pay all of your bills and obligations, buy all of your concert tickets, and fund all of your vacations. Then, at the end of the month, send us whatever you have left over." One thing's for sure. We'd have a lot fewer bureaucrats!

Whatever the government might be, it isn't dumb. It knows, full well, that if it waited to get its cut until after you paid your bills, its work would be in desperate straits. There would be nothing left over for it, just like there is nothing left over for you right now. And what do you do to compensate for this reduction in your income, compliments of Uncle Sam? You adjust your living standards to fit within the amount that is left over (hopefully).

What would happen if, the next time you received your check, you said, "You know, I can't afford to pay taxes anymore. I need that money for next month's trip to Hawaii." It wouldn't be long before you found yourself living with a new friend named Rocko, in a ten-by-ten cement room with steel windows, with no more worries about paying taxes (or monthly bills for that matter).

People pay taxes, and they pay them out of the *first dollars* they earn.

Why do you treat Uncle Sam better than you treat yourself? You don't intentionally; it's just that you don't think of it in those terms. The key to investment success is to do for yourself what the government so kindly does for you. Set aside a percentage of your income, and *save it right off of the top.* And the best way to do that is to treat that amount just like your taxes or any other bill. Pay it first and automatic deduction is best.

Ten percent may seem like an impossible amount, but it isn't. You may be surprised to find you don't even miss it. At least that much money filters through most people's fingers each month on things like coffee, fast food, and trinkets they don't need. Why? Simply because the money is there, begging to be spent. If you take it away first and create a false sense of scarcity, I don't believe you will lessen your standard of living one bit. You will just reduce the number of goodies you need to sell at your next garage sale.

When you are tempted to spend from your new savings account or to fudge just a little – don't! Pretend your investment money is just as impossible to access as the taxes you pay each and every month. If things are truly tight, plan your budget around this newly reduced amount. It may mean that you have to reevaluate your budget and cut something out that is not a necessity, but it is my experience that you will hardly notice the difference.

This has always been my motto: It's a lot easier to spend money that you've over-saved than it is to save money that you've over-spent.

Step 3: Start Today and Be Consistent

The last step is very simple – start today and don't waver from your plan. I'm going to address this in more detail in the following chapter.

Just to recap, these are the three simple steps to building and implementing a workable plan:

Step 1: Set a goal.

Step 2: Pay yourself first.

Step 3: Start today and be consistent.

Chapter 4

Landmine 2 – Procrastination

In the last chapter you saw, by our investment table, how dramatic an effect the percent of return can have on the future outcome of your investment. In this chapter we will look at the other significant factor in determining the size of your future nest egg – time.

"In 1626, Native Americans sold what is now called Manhattan Island, New York, to white settlers for a pile of trinkets worth only $24. Manhattan's value as real estate is now appraised at $23.4 billion. But if the Native Americans had sold those trinkets for $24 cash and placed the money in a 6% compound-interest account, their investment would now total $27,600,000,000. And if today's Native Americans had inherited this fortune, they could buy back Manhattan and still have over $4 billion left in their account!

That isn't to say the Native Americans got a fair deal, but rather to illustrate what seems like a little bit might be a lot more than you thought. In other words, great accomplishments don't necessarily require a huge initial investment, the talent of a genius, an incredible windfall, or a superhuman effort. Great accomplishments are possible for anyone who can muster just a little bit and then keep at it with persistence."[iv]

And that was a quote from 20 years ago. Now, at a continued rate of 6% interest, that $27,600,000,000 would be worth $88.5 billion.

Let me illustrate another way the power that time has on your investment. If, on the day Benjamin Franklin was born in 1706, his parents had deposited one cent into an account earning 8%, Mr. Franklin's heirs would now have a windfall of over $248 million, 311 years later.

The point is clear – *time has a huge effect on your investment.* Twenty-four dollars becomes $88.5 billion and $.01 turns into over $248 million. Of course, these time periods are much longer than our personal life expectancies, but it is important to know that you can harness this same power and put it to work for you during your lifetime.

Let me tell you one last story. It's a story about two individuals named Jill and Mark. At age 19 Jill started investing $2,000 a year into an account with a compound interest rate of 10%. After only eight years (age 26) she stopped investing and left her $16,000 to grow until age 65.

Mark on the other hand, because of life's demands, waited until he was 27 years old (the year Jill stopped) to begin saving for his retirement. He was still young and was proud of his early start and attention to his financial wellbeing. He also contributed $2,000 per year to his retirement, but he contributed for *39 years* – each year from age 27 until the year he retired at age 65. His total contribution over those 39 years was $78,000. (He started only eight years after Jill but contributed $62,000 more dollars.)

The big question is this: "Who had more money at retirement?" If you said Jill, you'd be right. The value of her investment at age 65 was $1,035,160, while Mark's was only $883,185. See figure 4.1.

| | JILL | | MARK | |
AGE	CONTRIBUTION	YEAR-END VALUE	CONTRIBUTION	YEAR-END VALUE
19	$2,000	$2,200	-$0-	-$0-
20	$2,000	$4,620	-$0-	-$0-
21	$2,000	$7,282	-$0-	-$0-
22	$2,000	$10,210	-$0-	-$0-
23	$2,000	$13,431	-$0-	-$0-
24	$2,000	$16,974	-$0-	-$0-
25	$2,000	$20,872	-$0-	-$0-
26	$2,000	$25,159	-$0-	-$0-
27	-$0-	$27,675	$2,000	$2,200
28	-$0-	$30,442	$2,000	$4,620
29	-$0-	$33,487	$2,000	$7,282
30	-$0-	$36,835	$2,000	$10,210
31	-$0-	$40,519	$2,000	$13,431
32	-$0-	$44,571	$2,000	$16,974
33	-$0-	$49,028	$2,000	$20,872
34	-$0-	$53,930	$2,000	$25,159
35	-$0-	$59,323	$2,000	$29,875
36	-$0-	$65,256	$2,000	$35,062
37	-$0-	$71,781	$2,000	$40,769
38	-$0-	$78,960	$2,000	$47,0415
39	-$0-	$86,856	$2,000	$53,950
40	-$0-	$95,541	$2,000	$61,545
41	-$0-	$105,095	$2,000	$69,899
42	-$0-	$115,605	$2,000	$79,089
43	-$0-	$127,165	$2,000	$89,198
44	-$0-	$139,882	$2,000	$100,318
45	-$0-	$153,870	$2,000	$112,550
46	-$0-	$169,257	$2,000	$126,005
47	-$0-	$186,183	$2,000	$140,805
48	-$0-	$204,801	$2,000	$157,086
49	-$0-	$225,281	$2,000	$174,995
50	-$0-	$247,809	$2,000	$194,694
51	-$0-	$272,590	$2,000	$216,364
52	-$0-	$299,849	$2,000	$240,200
53	-$0-	$329,834	$2,000	$266,420
54	-$0-	$362,834	$2,000	$295,262

Figure 4.1

	JILL		MARK	
AGE	CONTRIBUTION	YEAR-END VALUE	CONTRIBUTION	YEAR-END VALUE
55	-$0-	399,099	$2,000	$326,988
56	-$0-	$439,009	$2,000	$361,887
57	-$0-	$482,918	$2,000	$400,276
58	-$0-	$531,201	$2,000	$442,503
59	-$0-	$584,321	$2,000	$488,953
60	-$0-	$642,753	$2,000	$540,049
61	-$0-	$707,028	$2,000	$596,254
62	-$0-	$777,731	$2,000	$658,079
63	-$0-	$855,504	$2,000	$726,079
64	-$0-	$941,054	$2,000	$800,896
65	**-$0-**	**$1,035,160**	**$2,000**	**$883,185**

Figure 4.1 (continued)

You may be scratching your head saying, "Wait a minute. How can that be?" The answer is simple – *the amazing power of time* in the compound-interest equation. It truly is astounding, isn't it?

After that last example you may be thinking, "Oh great. I'm 43 years old and haven't done anything to save for my future. It's all over. There's no hope."

Don't get discouraged. It's never too late to begin. If you take advantage of the principles of this book and put yourself in a position to harvest tax-free dollars in retirement, you can supercharge your retirement years by avoiding tens of thousands – if not hundreds of thousands – of dollars of tax that can then be assimilated into *your* budget, instead of going to line the eternally voracious bureaucratic coffers.

Let me ask you another question. If you wanted a nice, big oak tree in your front yard, when would have been the best time to plant it? Certainly a hundred years ago or more, right? However, if that tree had never been planted, when would be the next best time to plant it? You got it – today!

This same principle holds true in the world of investing. When would have been the best time to start saving? The day you were born. But unless you were an exceptionally gifted infant, like the one in the television commercials, it probably didn't happen (unless of course a parent or grandparent was wise enough to know this principle). So just like the oak tree, if you haven't started saving yet, the best time to begin is right now – today!

If it makes so much sense to start early, why do people wait? Because life is geared that way. When you're in your twenties, thirties, and even forties, life throws you demand after demand, all of them urgent. It's a time when people are trying to get established and find their path. They start their career, get married, add children to their family, buy their first house, put new tires on their ten-year-old Chevy, put braces on junior number two, buy a car for junior number one, and a hundred-and-one other things that distract them from beginning to save for their future. Their need for money is right now. Life is expensive and saving becomes only a dream. Therefore, many people put off investing until that mythical "someday" when they have more money. Yet in most cases that "someday" never comes. Life's demands have a way of increasing faster than one's income. There is only one way to break this cycle. We addressed it in Step 2 in the last chapter – pay yourself first!

Maybe now you can see why I am taking the time to walk you carefully through these landmines before I introduce you to the powerful strategy that will allow you to build tax-free wealth. If you don't have this foundation in place, you could easily step on one of these hidden explosives and find yourself financially crippled. Without this foundation the profits from this new strategy won't mean a thing. You'll spend them, waste them, or assimilate them into your already overstuffed budget. You'll do anything but actually save them.

Thankfully, unlike tax-qualified retirement plans, you can begin the strategy I am going to present to you at *any* age. I started it for each of my four children when each was under a year old. Unlike most (if not all) other tax-advantaged vehicles, this strategy will allow you to harness the principle in this chapter – time – unlike any other vehicle in the investment marketplace that I'm aware of because not only can you begin it for a child during their first year of life, but there is also not an age at which you must stop investing or start withdrawing. And the combination of starting earlier and running longer can have dramatic effects upon the strategy's overall result.

As you can hopefully see, this chapter is not just a minor formality for the *Tax-Free Retirement*™ strategy; it is the very foundation for true financial success. For me to present the *Tax-Free Retirement*™ idea to you without showing you how to tiptoe carefully through the field of hidden *Financial Landmines*™ would be like sending a battalion of new recruits into battle without a battle plan. They would be doomed to certain death and so would your finances.

I hope, by the time you finish reading these landmines, you too will feel as strongly about them as I do. Please don't give in to the temptation to jump ahead without taking the time to plan appropriately – your financial success depends on it.

Chapter 5

Landmine 3 – Getting on the Wrong Side of Mr. Interest

Let me tell you a story about a man named Mr. Interest.[v] As a matter of fact, you know this individual. He's your employee, and he works for you around the clock. While you sleep. While you work. While you're on vacation.

He's the hardest worker who has ever lived, and he works for you. The question is, "What have you employed him to do?" Have you hired him to work *for* you or is he spending every second of every day working *against* you?

He can be your servant, whose free services profit you richly, or he can be an incessant bill collector, whose sole job is to charge you a wage, twenty-four hours a day, seven days a week, 365 days a year.

Which will it be?

In my profession I get the opportunity to work with many different business owners. Some are productive. Some are not. Some present themselves professionally. Some do not. Some have a vision for their future. Some do not. But one common denominator I've found in *every* business is this – employing good quality, faithful workers, who contribute to profit, is essential.

Employing Mr. Interest to work for you is like hiring a person to come to work, make you money, but never accept a paycheck. On the other hand hiring Mr. Interest to work against you is like paying an employee, every day of the year (including weekends and holidays), to run your business into the ground and give all your profits away to the competitor.

You definitely want to be on the right side of Mr. Interest.

Let me put this principle into concrete terms. I know an individual – I'll call him John – whose dream was to have a boat large enough to take out for a week or more at a time. It didn't need to be extravagant, just big enough to explore the great waters of the San Juan Islands and into Canada. After years of waiting the day finally arrived.

John's credit union told him he would have no problem qualifying for a loan. He scoured newspapers, boat magazines, and boat dealerships for good deals, and finally, one day, he found it. He found the boat he'd been dreaming about for years. And he did what any healthy, red-blooded American would do. He bought it – on credit, of course. The boat's final sticker price with tax and licensing came to about $43,000 – modest by all boating standards. John took out a ten-year loan, to keep the payments to a minimum, at an interest rate of 7.75%. (This was in the 1990s.) It was a good deal, to be sure, and he knew the memories he would build with his family would be worth every penny. But what John didn't fully understand was that at the very moment he inked the deal, Mr. Interest punched in on the time clock and began his relentless crusade against him.

You see, the memories John would build with his family would be far more costly than $43,000. Far more. Let me illustrate.

John's monthly payment for the boat was about $520 a month. Once he added in moorage, maintenance, fuel, and insurance, his monthly payments averaged out to be around $800 per month. He knew all of these figures even before he purchased the boat. They were costs he was happy to pay to fulfill a life-long dream.

However, John hadn't figured in the billing fee of Mr. Interest. When I sat down with him, I ran some numbers for him. Numbers he was shocked to see. I took that $800 per month and figured out how much John was going to pay for this dream boat, over the next ten years, at 7.75% interest. That figure came to $96,813.82. Okay, so his $43,000 boat was going to cost him a little more than $43,000. The family memories were still worth $100,000 he figured, more in an attempt to pacify his growing angst. However, I pointed out to him that this cost was only a *fraction* of Mr. Interest's actual bill.

"John, you may pay $96,813 for the boat, but how much would you have accumulated if you had saved that money for your retirement?"

"I have no idea," he said. So with the assistance of my financial calculator, we set off to find the answer.

"What do you feel is a reasonable average growth rate to expect on your money between now and your retirement?"

"I don't know. Does 12% seem too high? That seems like a number I've heard kicked around before." (It is important to note that this conversation happened in the 1990s, in the midst of the booming tech markets. At that time a growth rate of 12% actually seemed realistic to some individuals. In today's low-interest environment, however, a 12% growth rate seems preposterous.)

I explained to him that 12% was pretty aggressive, but for illustration sake I was happy to proceed with his suggestion.

"Okay. If you put that same $800 into a savings vehicle (whose accumulation does not get taxed) for 10 years, and you averaged a 12% return, you would amass a savings of $184,030.95."

"Wow!" he said, his eyes the size of small saucers.

"John, how many years do you plan to work?"

"Oh, I'd say another 35 years or so."

"Okay. We have already calculated the cost for the first 10 years. But if we want to see what that boat is actually costing you, we need to figure out how that amount will compound over the next 25 years. We want to know what that boat payment is actually costing you in retirement dollars."

"I'd never thought of it that way."

"Don't feel badly. Most people don't," I said consolingly. "Now, if we take that $184,030.95 and project its growth over the next 25 years at 12%, without adding another penny, we come up with a total cost of $3,641,690.25."

Now not only were his eyes the size of saucers, but the tremor of his lower jaw hitting my desk measured a 6.0 on the Richter Scale.

"You've got to be kidding! My $43,000 worth of family memories is really costing me over $3,500,000 in retirement savings? I love my family, but I had no idea how much this dream was really costing me!"

"Yep," I said, letting the numbers speak for themselves.

"I can't get over the fact that a $40,000 boat is actually costing me millions of dollars!"

"You now see the importance of being on the right side of Mr. Interest," I said.

"No kidding. If I invested the money that I am now spending on the boat, I could easily pay cash for the boat later and still have a lot left over."

"Now you're getting the idea," I said. But unfortunately, I wasn't finished with John; I had to dig the knife a little deeper. "John, I hate to be the bearer of bad news, but it's even worse than the picture we've already painted."

"What do you mean?" he said.

I wanted to take John down the next path that most people never travel and show him how money that is heavily taxed upon withdrawal will make these numbers even more grim.

"John, right now, where are you saving money?"

"I was putting $1,000 a month into my 401(k) at work, but I'm reducing that amount to $200 so I can buy this boat. I decided the dream was worth it. At least I thought it was before this conversation."

"So if you weren't buying that boat, you would be continuing to fund your 401(k)?" I asked.

"Yes."

"Do you realize that once you start taking money out of that account, every penny is taxed as income?"

"Sort of. I never really stopped to think about it. All I know is that I get the tax write off today. I like that."

"Sure you do. We all like saving money on our taxes. But you are not really *saving* money on your taxes; you are simply *delaying and compounding* the problem."

"What do you mean?"

"Well, in very simplistic terms, if that $3,500,000 was in an account you could access tax-free, how much of *your* money would be in that account?"

"I'm sure I'm missing the point, because it seems too obvious. I'd say three-and-a-half million."

"No tricks here. You are tracking well, and you're correct. You'd have the full three and a half million."

Then I posed the next question to him. "If you accumulate that same amount of money in your 401(k) or other tax-qualified retirement plan, how much of your money is in that account?

"Okay, now I'm really starting to worry, but I'd say the same amount. You just said I would have that much in the account, so why would this be any different?"

"You're right, partially," I said. "Your account statement would read $3,500,000, but is that what *you* would really have?"

"Obviously not, by the way you're asking the question, but I'm not sure I follow."

"Who else has a stake in your retirement account?"

"No one. It's just in my name."

I was starting to smile as I said, "That's not entirely true. You see, since every penny in your account needs to be taxed upon withdrawal, the IRS could be nearly a 40% stakeholder in your account. And that's not counting any potential state taxes you might incur. Actually, since we don't know what tax rates will do in the future, that number could be lower, or it could be drastically higher. But let's assume the tax rate on the funds to be roughly 40%, just to be safe." Now my smile was fully engaged. "Did you know you were saving money for Uncle Sam's retirement?"

Obviously, no one had ever really explained to John what would happen to his tax-qualified retirement plan in the distribution phase, because he sat there without saying a word, slipping into a financial depression before my very eyes. I decided I'd better finish quickly, in order to throw him a life ring before he sunk completely.

"John, I'm telling you this for two reasons. One, most people don't understand this, and in the later years they find themselves burdened with excessive taxes they didn't need to pay. The good news is that I can show you a different way, so you can begin saving 100% of your retirement account for *you* and not let Uncle Sam touch one penny upon withdrawal, at least based on today's current tax laws.

"The second reason is to show you the power of this other strategy. You see, in order to accumulate $3,500,000 of *your* money inside your tax-qualified plan, you would need to amass just over $5,800,000. Why? Because Uncle Sam gets his 40% cut upon withdrawal. However, if you use this new strategy, then you can keep the full account value and realize the entire amount for yourself. So to completely depress you, that fiberglass palace of family memories is actually costing you somewhere between $3,500,000 and $5,800,000, depending on how wise you are with your saving choices."

"Yes, Patrick, you have depressed me, but I think I'll recover pretty quickly," he said, with a chuckle of his own, as he picked up his phone. "One thing is for sure. You have opened my eyes to some pretty interesting ideas. How come no one else has told me these things?"

Once again, I was faced with the perennial question that only had one answer. "John, as weird as it sounds, the only reasonable answer I can come up with is that most of the so-called financial 'professionals' may not really understand these concepts either."

I had hardly finished my last sentence before John was dialing the number to a local yacht broker, asking him to sell his multi-million-dollar dream boat.

For the first time in his life, John fully understood that time is indeed money, for that is what allows Mr. Interest to work his true magic.

Before I conclude this chapter, I want to clarify a couple of important issues. There is *nothing* wrong with owning a boat. There is nothing wrong with desiring to build lasting memories with your family. And there is actually nothing wrong with buying a big-ticket item on credit. It's all up to you. But beware. There *is* something wrong with not fully understanding the power of Mr. Interest.

Money is not the most important thing in life. Far from it. This example was not given to entice you to sell everything you own and hoard money for your future savings. Rather, this story was shared simply to illustrate the incredible power of compound interest and how much it can cost you to be on the wrong side of our friend or foe, Mr. Interest.

Chapter 6

Landmine 4 – Desire for Instant Gratification

In America having to wait feels like contracting a disease. Think about what has happened to our society over the last twenty years. Take banks for example. First they added a drive-up window, so their customers wouldn't have to take the time to get out of their cars. Obviously, that wasn't quite good enough, so cash machines were added for even faster service. But that, too, must have been inconvenient, because soon after that came the advent of the drive-through-cash-machine. However, that wasn't the end of the line either, because now banks offer the ultimate efficiency in banking and allow you to make all your transactions on the telephone or via the internet any time of the day, any day of the week.

But banks are just one example. Think about the other revolutions we have made in the art of instant gratification. A leisurely sit-down meal has become a grease bomb at a drive-through burger joint. Someone with seven items in the express lane at the grocery store has almost become justification for a lawsuit. And going shopping requires nothing more than a few clicks on a keyboard.

We, as Americans, loathe anything that causes us to slow down our frantic pursuit. We hate lines. We hate traffic jams. And we hate paying cash.

Cash represents spending money we actually possess. And the concept of spending only the money we earn is labeled as prehistoric thinking. We have home loans and car loans and business loans and boat loans and credit card loans. And then when our loan ratio is about ready to burst at the seams, we take out loans to pay our loans. We use our Mastercard® to pay our Visa®. If we can't afford it, we charge it. The thought of paying cash is a thing of the past – but it doesn't have to be.

I heard on the radio back in 2002 that credit card companies were sending out two and a half billion applications every year – that's an average of twenty-five applications for every man, woman, and child in America. I can only imagine what that number is today. When you consider that many of the people in our country never receive a single one of these applications, that means some people (like you and me) receive over one hundred of these irritating applications every year. The financial world has not only made it possible for Americans to crank up their debt, they expect it. How can someone with a lust for more turn down the offer for "free" money one hundred times a year? The answer is simple. They can't.

Right after I heard this statistic back in 2002, I performed a small experiment. Instead of throwing away all the credit card offers I received in the mail, I decided to keep them and see just how much credit I could potentially accumulate if I wanted to. I was going to do this for an entire year, but I couldn't. I had to quit. The sheer volume was utterly ridiculous; I had to dedicate an entire file drawer to holding all these credit card offers. I averaged about four offers per week, each one offering a credit line of $10,000 or more.

If you put a calculator to those numbers, which are conservative at best, you come up with substantially more than $2,000,000. Can you believe it? I don't know how many of those a person could get issued, but it is safe to say that many Americans could secure tens (and possibly hundreds) of thousands of dollars in credit card potential, in a period of twelve short months. If that isn't a temptation for someone lacking moral integrity, I don't know what is. That person could throw the party of the century, live high on the hog for years, travel the world, buy all sorts of expensive toys, and just when the clock was about to strike midnight and Cinderella's coach was ready to turn back into a pumpkin, that person could spend a few measly bucks with a local attorney, file bankruptcy, and wipe the slate clean. No criminal charges. No legal ramifications. Just a slap on the hand and a bad credit rating for seven years. If you think I'm making this up, think again. Thousands and thousands of people did exactly this, and we called it the Credit Crisis, which began to take hold of the financial world back in late 2008. And while banks' lending regulations may have changed since then, I'm not so sure that consumers' habits have. I see as much debt and borrowing going on today as I did before the Credit Crisis gripped the world in its stranglehold.

Is it any wonder that people are in financial trouble? Most folks are way over their head in consumer debt. And the big question is: Why? No one likes being in debt. No one likes credit card balances. So why do the masses do it? The answer is simple – people don't like to wait. The motto of our time is, "I want it, and I want it now." Waiting to purchase something is for those financial weaklings who can't get a credit card.

But what these people don't realize is that they unknowingly have one foot poised over a deadly explosive. The desire for instant gratification is a lethal, financial landmine. And it is not choosy whom it destroys. Its effects can be merely crippling, but more often than not, they're lethal.

So how do you avoid the fate of this deadly foe? *Think before you spend*! And only spend what you have in your bank account, *not* what you have on your credit limit.

Does that mean you can't buy a home on credit? No. Does that mean it is wrong to finance a brand new car? No. But I give you a strong warning against car loans and other consumer debt of any kind. Be careful. This kind of debt is a dangerous landmine we're talking about, not some child's toy.

Debt is the budget item that eats up most people's savings. It is a financial anchor chained tightly around their legs. People find themselves not being able to save, because they've become enslaved. Enslaved to the debt that has resulted from their passion to buy things right now – today. Not only does this lifestyle have a crippling effect on their future savings, it is also devastating to any chance of maintaining a healthy, financial morale. These people are always the proverbial "day late and dollar short." They are always paying off yesterday's purchases instead of saving for tomorrow's needs.

Be careful of this reverse planning! However, if this message has reached you a little too late, and you find you've already accumulated more debt than you can pay off, I encourage you to do something very un-American. Are you ready?

Step 1: March into your kitchen or den and grab a pair of sharp scissors.

Step 2: Proceed to remove all of your credit cards – yes all of them – from your wallet or purse.

Step 3: Next, take those sharp scissors and cut every one of those little pieces of plastic to shreds.

Step 4: Now, stand up and march out of the room chanting at the top of your lungs, "No more debt! No more debt! No more debt!"

Step 5: Enjoy the unexpected feeling of freedom you now experience.

Maybe step four seems a bit excessive, but I'm totally serious about the others. If you do this you will help ensure that you will not put yourself further into debt. However, unfortunately it does nothing to remedy the poor spending choices of your past. But don't despair. You will find that once you begin to spend only the money you make and are not progressively digging yourself deeper and deeper into debt, you will be able to allocate more money each month to paying your existing loans or saving for your future.

As you work to bring your spending into check – think! Ask yourself if you really need the item you desire or if it's just a fleeting want. These fleeting wants are what usually end up collecting dust in our garage.

One conservative financial author takes this idea a step further and encourages people to develop a "want-list" for large ticket items. You get to define large for yourself. For some it may be $50. For others it may be $500. This "want-list" is a very short list because it can only contain *one* item at a time. And that one item must stay on this list for 90 days before the purchase is made. What usually happens, he says, is that sometime during that 90-day period he finds an item he wants more than the one on the list. So he replaces it. But once he does that, the 90-day clock starts all over again. This has protected him from making many unnecessary and unwanted purchases.[vi]

Something different may work for each one of us, but the principles are the same:

- Spend less than you earn.
- Don't buy on impulse.
- Resist your desire for instant gratification.

Chapter 7

Landmine 5 – Following the Masses

In J.D. Salinger's book *The Catcher in the Rye*, the main character, Holden Caulfield, has a dream. In this dream he pictures many children running through a tall field of rye. However, unbeknownst to the children, they are running straight toward a deadly cliff that sinisterly waits for them at the far side of the field.

This scene is not unlike the investment climate in our world today. The average person saving for retirement is running through a field of tax-qualified retirement plans without the knowledge of what lurks on the other side. They are running carefree, enjoying the beauty of the day, content with life as they know it. But things are about to change. The pleasure of today's tax write-offs will soon materialize as tomorrow's tax nightmares, and the sunny day which they are now enjoying will soon darken with the storm clouds of tomorrow's tax burdens. Everything is about to change. The cliff is coming. And the masses don't have a clue.

Why shouldn't we follow the masses? I'll make this very simple. *The masses are usually wrong.* Let's look at the history of the stock market for a little example. If you look throughout history, what do the masses usually do? Just the opposite of what they should. They buy when they should be selling, and they sell when they should be buying. The masses act on instinct, but most financial markets don't. They require a reverse kind of instinct. One that runs contrary to our inborn nature.

And who are the masses? You know them well. It's you and me, your neighbor next door, your co-worker in the next cubicle, the person in your golf foursome or carpool. If you look at the history of the stock market, by nature, most of us do it wrong. And we do it wrong because of two basic human instincts – fear and greed. These two instincts are also helped along by the innate desire for us to be like everyone else. We want to be liked. We don't want to stand out. The bottom line is that we want to be like everyone else. It's a cycle we must break if we want to achieve the great things that are possible.

Most people saving for retirement need to revisit their kindergarten class and hear their teachers remind them that just because little Johnny stuck a piece of macaroni up his nose, doesn't mean that we should stick one up our nose as well.

There are certainly times when it is better *not* to follow the lead of others. Kindergarten was one; investing in government-sponsored, tax-qualified plans may be another.

In reading this book *Tax-Free Retirement*™, I want you to realize that you no longer need to blindly follow the masses simply because it is the only path through the field of rye. I want everyone to know that an alternative *does* exist that can potentially exceed the benefits of today's tax-qualified retirement plans. The secret has been kept too long. Someone owes you an apology. An apology for robbing you of the knowledge that has been utilized by the privileged few for decades.

Before you continue to run blindly any longer, stop and evaluate your situation. Study the coming chapters in this book. Then decide, on your own, what is best for *your* financial future. Stop throwing your money away along with the masses. You don't want to suffer as a result of their ignorance.

Chapter 8

Landmine 6 – The Inertia Factor

Let me give you a warning. I have seen this happen numerous times, and it will probably happen again with you as you read this book. You are going to go through what I call the "discovery cycle." Near the end of this "discovery cycle" lies a large temptation. The temptation to *do nothing* – to read this book and then put it down without allowing yourself to change. Though we don't like to admit it, it is often easier for us to do the things we know than it is to try something new, even if a new way is more profitable.

If my guess is correct, right now you are sensing a new excitement about your financial future. And you should. The information that is yet to come is exciting. However, if you don't overcome the *Inertia Factor*, nothing will change.

I can still remember learning about inertia in my high school physics class. Simply put, it is the energy necessary to get an object in motion. All of us have an inertia point. Think about it.

Why do we get out of bed each morning and go to work? We do so because we need to earn money to buy food, obtain shelter, and to enjoy whatever other things our paycheck provides. Therefore, we can conclude that the desire to have these things provides enough inertia for us to get up each morning and keep a job, instead of staying home and zoning in front of television re-runs.

Everything you do has an associated inertia factor. Investing is no different. You can read this book and be as charged up as a Virginia firefly, but unless you act on this knowledge, the excitement is purely wasted. It profits you nothing.

And let me assure you, there are many idea junkies out there who get a good buzz off of a new idea. They don't have to use it; they just have to learn it. Don't be an idea junkie. Instead, find something that works and focus your energy on that one thing. Instead of trying to put your eggs in different baskets, as we have so often been told to do, it might be better to put them all in one basket and then watch that basket very, very carefully. You see, diversification of our investments is wise, but diversification of our energy is foolish. We can't be a master of all things and expect exceptional returns.

I include this seemingly innocuous landmine in this book because the strategies you are about to learn in the upcoming chapters require action on your part in order to set them into motion. Minor action... but action nonetheless. Very few saving strategies are easier to set up or maintain than the one I am going to introduce you to. As a matter of fact, if it is done correctly, it should take almost no time on your part to manage. Having said that, it does still take the initial effort – effort that could potentially save you hundreds of thousands of dollars in taxes in the future.

Resist the temptation to reject what is new or different. Be willing to act when you discover a fantastic opportunity like the one I'm going to introduce to you in the pages to come. Don't let the *Inertia Factor* force you back into doing the same things you've always done.

I'm sure you've heard the saying, "If you always do what you've always done, you'll always get what you've always got."

It's true.

I hope you will use this book to launch yourself into action in order to propel yourself down a life-long road of successful savings.

Chapter 9

Landmine 7 – A Desire to Get Rich Quick

I can only wonder how many fortunes have been lost and families have been ruined by the greed-driven desire to get rich quickly. This mentality has been elevated to epidemic proportions. Everywhere I turn I see its mark on our society – television's infamous infomercials, lottery tickets sold weekly by the millions, and the endless offers that appear in my mailbox, tempting me with innumerable assurances that I will make my fortune in the next three to six months.

Over the last 20 years, with the rise of tech behemoths like Microsoft, Apple, Amazon, Google, and many others, we have witnessed a season in which stock options created over-night millionaires – individuals who could retire after as few as five years of work, having done nothing more than work for the right company at the right time. These instant millionaires caused the rest of society to feel left behind; therefore, many people tried other means to keep up with Mr. "Stock Option" Jones.

Living, for some people, has become nothing more than a sport – the ultimate competition. Many live by the axiom that I've seen paraded above the tailpipe of many cars, "He who dies with the most toys wins."

People buy lottery tickets by the hundreds. They cross their fingers and roll dice in Vegas. They play the horses at their local track. They follow the stock suggestions of self-professed financial gurus. They buy stakes in ostrich farms in Oregon and oil fields in South America. And they gamble their money away in financial markets they know absolutely nothing about – all to make a fast buck.

Let me assure you of one thing. Except for a very small percentage of people, and I mean *very* small (who happen to be both lucky and good), these methods provide only one thing – a sure road to financial ruin.

How can you protect yourself from falling prey to the get-rich-quick tactics that assault you from every angle? (And you can be certain there will be times when an offer looks so good that the temptation will be hard to refuse.) Here are two simple principles to follow.

Invest in What You Know

It is tempting to discover a new opportunity and assume there is an untouched pot of gold just waiting to be taken. You think to yourself, *who better to do the taking than me*? The problem is that each opportunity has a different set of rules. Far too many people, looking to bypass the natural method of building wealth, set out after a new pot of gold without realizing they don't have a clue what they're doing. They are throwing money at something they hope will pay great dividends, like a novice gambler hoping to get lucky enough to draw the right card.

Avoid these get-rich-quick temptations. Invest your money in things you can trust – things that are easy to understand and that have been around for decades and which are familiar to you. And don't trust anyone who tells you they have a "for-sure deal." You may hit it lucky a few times, but eventually you will end up in the poor house.

By the time you are done reading this book, you will find that the *Tax-Free Retirement*™ strategy meets this criteria very well. It is a time-tested method that is easy to execute and available to most everyone, month after month, year after year.

Remember – The Tortoise Beat the Hare

I said it early in this book, and I'll say it again – slow and steady wins the race. Remember the tortoise in the childhood story *The Tortoise and the Hare*? Mr. Hare took off like a shot, blowing the tortoise away, right from the starting blocks. He was so confident of his abilities that he afforded himself many leisurely stops along the way, distracting himself from his ultimate goal.

In contrast, Mr. Tortoise knew his physical limitations, so to compensate he just kept at it – hour after hour. He kept plodding toward the goal that awaited him, and sure enough, his persistence paid off. He won the race. He didn't win it because he was the fastest runner. He won it because his personal discipline kept him focused on the goal, and he didn't let himself get distracted by all the temptations along the way. In simplest terms, he just kept at it.

I believe this story holds great significance in the area of personal investing. If you follow the plan laid out in the previous chapters, as well as the ones to come, all you need to do is keep plugging away at your goal. Don't get sidetracked by some tempting offer that is too good to be true. Almost always, it's exactly that – too good to be true.

Create a simple and achievable plan and then pursue that plan. Let others throw their money to the wind, if they choose to, while yours is diligently working to increase your long-term wealth.

Chapter 10

Landmine 8 – Lack of Generosity

I remember learning a valuable lesson the year after I graduated from college. I can still recall with clarity the lazy Saturday morning I received the phone call. I probably remember it so well because it was the first one of its kind I had ever received since I had embarked on true, post-college bachelorhood. The call was nothing special. It was a cold call – a solicitation. I'm sure I was chosen at random from a phone directory. But I didn't know that at the time.

I don't remember the lady's name, but she was a financial planner at a large company in downtown Seattle. She was calling to see if I would like to come in to her office for a free financial analysis.

I didn't want to waste her time, so I felt the need to give her a clear picture of my meager financial situation. I had just graduated from college and was working as a youth pastor in a local church, making a whopping $15,000 per year. I had little money to live on, let alone *plan* with.

Now as I look back, it really was a humorous scene. I'm sure she was a new recruit who had quotas to fill. Here I was earning an income probably below the poverty level, but she didn't miss a beat. No matter how many times I tried to tell her that I really didn't have any money to plan with, she just assured me that it was all the more reason we needed to meet. Finally, for some odd reason, I gave in. I believe the reason I did was because I was naïve to the entire cold-call approach. I somehow believed I was one of the privileged few to receive such an offer. Besides, I would get a chance to see Seattle's financial district. But, whatever the reason, I went.

Our meeting was fairly brief. I filled out a financial questionnaire and answered numerous other questions as she scribbled answers on a yellow pad. As the questions wound down, I think she realized that all the creative ideas in the world couldn't make something out of nothing. I didn't have any pressing needs, but I didn't have any money to invest either. She looked at me and said, "I guess you were right. There isn't much I can do for you."

I remember chuckling and feeling a little foolish. Yet I had to remember it was only because of her insistence that I was there in the first place. But she did have a couple of comments for me before I left, and it was in these comments that I gathered a valuable piece of information.

She said, "Really, you have a very good handle on your finances. You have no debt and are able to budget the money you make to cover all of your monthly expenses. I also noticed that you give away ten percent of your income to charity. I have found that the people I meet with who give a set portion of their income to charity are also the best savers and money managers."

"That's interesting. Why is that?" I asked.

"Well, I'm not sure. I think it may be because they have an active plan for their finances. They are aware of what they make and where their money goes. All-in-all, they just seem to be the most successful financial managers I meet with."

"Thanks for the input," I said. "If I have a need for your services in the future, I'll give you a call."

We parted with pleasantries, and I was on my way, unaware that the simple conversation that concluded our meeting would stick with me many years later and make its way into a future book.

I believe she was right, and during my twenty-five years of helping clients with their money decisions, this fact has proven itself true time and time again. People who are generous with their money and enjoy giving to others, also find they are not usually lacking themselves. The Bible confirms this principle when it says, *"Remember this: Whoever sows sparingly will also reap sparingly, and whoever sows generously will also reap generously."vii* Think about it. It's true. If we smile at someone we pass on the street, they usually smile in return. If we give a compliment to someone, they usually proffer the same positive response. Likewise, if we shout at someone in anger, they usually shout back. Truly, we do find we reap what we sow. In other words we receive what we offer.

In a financial sense this doesn't mean we are going to get back some specific ratio of dollars for every dollar we give away, but somehow, people who give part of their income to others and live off of only 90% or less usually end up doing more with that 90% than other folks do with their 100%. They use the rest of their money more wisely and usually see more clearly the value of saving for the future.

Many people have short-circuited their finances by trying to hoard all of their money. Their shortsightedness has cost them dearly. If you are one of these individuals, I encourage you to take a step back from your present circumstances and re-evaluate the joy of being able to give part of your income away to your church or to those who are in need – kids without homes, adults without meals, people without hope.

Not only will you likely manage your finances better if you give part of your income away, but I guarantee you will also receive some rewards money can't buy – a sense of satisfaction, joy, and contentment that remains long after the money is forgotten.

For the benefit of others, as well as for your own financial wellbeing, I encourage you to begin to give. If you're married sit down with your spouse and decide where you would like to give part of your income. If you have children and they are of an appropriate age, include them in these discussions and decisions. What better way is there to pass on a generous spirit to your children than to have them be an active part of the family giving process?

While you're discussing these topics, it is also a great time for you to set some plans for your own savings goals and contributions. To reiterate this point, the better you are at giving away part of your resources, the better you will be at saving part of your resources. That is a true win-win situation.

Chapter 11

Landmine 9 - Acting Like the Future Will Never Arrive

This landmine is unique. It is really the place where the previous eight chapters come together in commonality. It is the glue that makes them stick.

Do you remember what it felt like, as a kid, to anticipate the arrival of Christmas day? The Thanksgiving feast was no sooner cleared off the table before you began to wonder, *when is Santa going to arrive*? That month between Thanksgiving and Christmas seemed like forever from your childhood perspective. But it always came. And once it arrived, you were sure it was only yesterday that you had been eating a holiday turkey and watching the Thanksgiving Day parade. The perspective looking forward always seems longer than the perspective looking back.

And so it will be in retirement.

All those years of work. All your anticipation. All those days where retirement seemed to be only an event in someone else's dreams. But before you know it, your time will be here. And once it is, you'll look back and say, "Wow, where did all the time go?"

We are not too different from children. We look at the future and act as if it will never arrive. Intellectually, we believe it will, but only *action* speaks our true belief. And according to all the recent studies I've read, the average American's actions toward saving for retirement are anemic at best.

During the 19th century there lived a dynamic tightrope-walker and showman named Charles Blondin. He was, undoubtedly, the greatest funambulist that ever lived. His thirst for new and daring stunts was unquenchable. In 1859, at the age of 35, he became the first person to cross Niagara Falls on a tightrope, 1100 feet long and 160 feet above the water. But just crossing this rope was not enough; history reports that Blondin accomplished this feat numerous times, always with different theatrical variations: blindfolded, in a sack, on stilts, carrying a man on his back, and sitting down midway while he cooked and ate an omelet.

Back and forth he went, dazzling the onlookers with his brilliant skill. They were amazed. He made every crossing without a hitch. One day, as the crowd gathered, he stepped off the wire, grabbed an empty wheelbarrow, and stepped back onto the perilous wire. Again, he proceeded to amaze the crowd as he pushed this wheelbarrow back and forth, high above the crashing falls.

After he made his way back to the crowd, he stepped off the tightrope a second time, looked straight at the astonished crowd, and asked this question: "Who believes I can walk across this wire with a wheelbarrow?" Every hand shot up. They had just witnessed his masterful feat.

While all the hands were still raised, he pointed at a young man in the front row and said, "Please, sir, get in the wheelbarrow."

Quickly the hands went down, including the young man's, as he slipped away through the crowd, escaping to safety. The problem was that the man's belief was only intellectual; otherwise, he would have stepped into Blondin's wheelbarrow.

You see, *true belief requires action*. It is action that gives belief its power. This is true in all areas of life. Yet most people's beliefs never venture out of the safe arena of intellect – an arena that requires no commitment and no action.

I tell you this story because it very closely parallels people's actions toward retirement. Intellectually, they plan to retire. Many even have the year marked on their mental calendar. But somewhere along the line this intellectual plan fails to turn into action. Every year retirement draws closer, and every year they put off the action of setting money aside because of some immediate need shouting very loudly for them to acquiesce.

We tend to forget the future. We believe it is an eternity away, just like we felt about Christmas as a child. But in the same way, it will be here before we know it. And once it arrives, if we didn't start saving soon enough, our only planning will be to figure out where we want to work until the day the mortician decides to give us our last hairstyle.

Don't fall into the trap of believing you have plenty of time before you need to start acting. Start now. The time will pass much more quickly than you think.

* * *

As I conclude this section of the book, I want to address one last, important issue, and I feel this is the most appropriate chapter in which to include these comments. I want to editorialize, briefly, on the entire subject of retirement so it doesn't seem like I am painting with too broad a brush.

This book appears to be making one huge assumption – that you plan to retire. Yet for many this may not be the case. I know many individuals who plan to work until either their health takes them out of the marketplace or they die. Many can't stand the thought of being idle. I, myself, am one of those individuals.

Let me take this opportunity to broaden your perspective of retirement. You see, I *do* plan to stop working simply to earn a living, but I *never* plan to stop working to contribute to society. For many people, retirement is seen as the long awaited rest after years of drudgery – a time to play after decades of servitude. That is okay. But it is not big enough for me. I want to spend my life doing what I love right now – not waiting until some future date that offers no guarantees. Retirement will simply allow me to pursue my dreams with greater freedom. It will be a chance to give myself completely to what I love without having to worry about providing an income. Retirement should be a time of liberation – a time to pursue your gifts and passions with a new sense of independence, a time to share your wisdom and availability with those who need it most. As a matter of fact, the first six chapters in my little book *Seven Secrets to a Happy Retirement* talk all about this.

When you hear the word retirement, what picture comes to mind? A gray-haired octogenarian whose body is tired from years of labor or a youthful-spirited individual, with a zest for life, who is just reaching his best years? Who says that retirement needs to take place at sixty-five? If you avoid these nine *Financial Landmines*™ and pursue the incredible opportunity that is awaiting you in the chapters to come, you may just find you have the option to retire years before you ever thought possible.

I don't know your personal situation, and I don't know your desires. But I do know it is wise to position yourself so that when you come to the point in your life where you want to retire, be it ten years or forty, you will have choices. And those choices will be the ones you desire, not ones forced upon you due to lack of planning.

PART III: THE HIDDEN RETIREMENT TRAPS

Chapter 12

A Story about Bill

I'd like to tell you a story about Bill. Bill is a fictitious 36 year old in upper management with a major corporation. However, it wouldn't matter if Bill was a physician, a small-business owner, a lawyer, a farmer, a teacher, or an employee of any company large or small. Although figures would differ, the story would be the same.

Bill's current annual salary is $150,000. This is the only company he's worked for since he graduated from college (with honors I might add), and in the fourteen years he has been with this company, he has worked his way up from the front lines due to his faithful and diligent effort. He arrives early and is often the last to leave. He's a company man whom everyone respects, and he's sought out for advice by those who report to him as well as his superiors.

Bill has been married to Marcy for nine years. Together they have three young children – Lauren 6, Tommy 4, and Scott 1.

He loves his kids, and though he doesn't get as much time with them as he would like, he wants what's best for them and is willing to help them in any way he can, including financially. He hopes each of them will study hard, go to college (a cost he is planning on paying as his father had for him), and find a solid job with a great company, just as he was fortunate to find. Secretly, Bill hopes that at least one of his kids might follow in his footsteps and become a future employee of his current company.

Bill's company has a wonderful 401(k) plan that he has contributed to, faithfully, since the beginning of his employment. When he first started with the company, he heard a presentation by a financial professional who told him the best place to invest his money was in his company's sponsored 401(k) for three reasons.

First, the presenter said that the company would match up to $1,500 per year. This was free money. All Bill had to do to receive it was contribute that amount himself, which sounded good to him. He'd take all the free money he could get.

The second reason he was told why this was the best place to save money for his future was that all the income he contributed was tax deferred. At 22 Bill didn't know what that really meant, but the individual went on to explain that all of the money he contributed would avoid tax in the year it was put into the plan. So if he made an annual income of $30,000 and contributed $1,500 to the 401(k), he would only be taxed on $28,500. And no tax was owed on the money until he took it out at retirement. The more he contributed, the more tax he would save.

The third reason the presenter gave him as to why this was such a great investment method was that when he began withdrawing money in retirement, he would be in a lower tax bracket. Since he would be in a lower tax bracket, he would pay less tax. Again, another exciting prospect in Bill's mind.

Bill had always been good at seeking advice from other professionals, so he went to see his CPA as well as one of the top executives of his company.

His CPA told him that investing in his company's 401(k) was a wonderful idea and that it would indeed lower his tax bill each year. He encouraged Bill to save as much as he could in his 401(k), even while his income was small.

The executive who he visited (a long-time family friend) gave him similar advice. He told Bill that the 401(k) had been the single best investment choice he had ever made. As a matter of fact, it was the only investment that had really made him money. The executive laughed out loud as he recalled some other investments he had made on "tips" from others – across the board all had been losers.

Bill was really excited to begin his investing career. He had done his homework, he had sought advice, he could avoid tax now, and he didn't have to a pay a penny in tax until he began to withdraw money from his account at a *lower* tax rate. What could be better than that?

After these two visits, Bill had made a commitment to contribute as much as he could afford to his 401(k), even if it meant he would have to stretch in other areas. During his fourteen years with the company, Bill had been a diligent saver and has accumulated $145,000 in his account. Since his income was meager in the early years, and the demands of his young family were growing, Bill was not able to contribute as much as he would have liked, but he is now proud of his growing nest egg. Now that his current income is much more significant, Bill is able to contribute the full maximum his retirement account will allow. At this rate and with this continued funding, his benefit statement shows a projected value of $2,669,414 at the age of 62, which is the year Bill hopes to retire. Since he is contributing so much to his 401(k), he is not able to save any additional money, including money toward his children's college education. This concerns Bill, but he figures that with his current income he and Marcy can cut back on some of their extra living expenses when the kids hit college and just pay for each year as the tuition comes due. Bill is 36, and he feels good about his financial future … a financial future that will come to greet him all too quickly.

Let's take a peek at his future, at least in some possible ways it might play out for this shrewd, hard-working individual.

Time has passed quickly. Bill is now 50, and his oldest daughter, Lauren, is a junior in college. It has been a great two years seeing his daughter flourish in a small, private university. He has contributed the maximum allowed to his 401(k) every year for the last 14 years. Bill is proud of his wise savings because his 401(k) now sits at $848,819… he is almost a millionaire.

However, the finances have been far tighter than Bill had expected. Although his income has blossomed to a whopping $259,751, a 4% increase each year, school costs have escalated far more quickly – at a rate of nearly 6%. That means what was once a $40,000 price tag for a year of private tuition (including room and board) now demands a whopping $90,000. He never imagined that one child's college tuition could demand almost 35% of his gross income and over 45% of his net income. Bill and Marcy have been scrambling for the last two years to try and pay for Lauren's tuition out of pocket, but it just isn't happening. They have managed to live right up to their increasing income. They have been able to make some cuts but not enough to pay the entire bill or even half of it for that matter. Bill doesn't want to tell Lauren that she can't continue attending the college of her dreams, so he knows he'll figure out a way to make it happen.

Bill and Marcy have tried looking into financial aid, but with Bill's healthy income they don't qualify. *How can anyone afford to send their kids to college?* Bill wonders.

After they had been rejected by the financial aid office, Bill decided to call the benefits department at his company to inquire about taking money out of his 401(k). Bill was told he cannot make an early withdrawal (before 59 ½) without paying tax on the money as ordinary income. Currently, Bill's federal income tax rate is 40%, his state income tax has risen to 10%, and on top of that he would have a 10% tax penalty for an early withdrawal. That means he would have to take $225,000 out of his 401(k) just to be able to pay a $90,000 tuition bill. Ludicrous! There is no way he is going to do that! That is 26.5% of his *entire* 401(k) for just one year of Lauren's tuition. Bill and Marcy have spent the last two years significantly cutting back on all the luxuries they had come to enjoy, but they believe their mission is worth the cost. Besides, it is only for a short season. They have stopped going out to fancy dinners; they have cancelled plans for nice family vacations for the next few years; they were advised to take out a second mortgage on their home; and Bill has even come to the conclusion that he will no longer be able to fund his 401(k), at least not until the kids are done with college and all their debts are paid – a decision he really dislikes.

Bill wonders to himself how he could be almost a millionaire on paper but feel flat broke. He has no access to his money without severe penalties. He feels like his own money is being held hostage by the tax system. But he has not worked so hard to sock money away for his retirement, only to find 60% of it gobbled up in taxes and penalties. A little thought passes through Bill's mind, and he wonders, for the first time, if his 401(k) really *has* been the best place to save money.

But Bill's financial concerns don't end here. This is also the year that Tommy is going to be a freshman in college. If one child has been a struggle, how in the world is he going to afford two kids in college? And still a third is not far behind. Bill sees only three options: 1. Tell the kids they need to get jobs to help pay for their own tuition. 2. Tell the kids they need to go to less expensive schools. 3. Borrow more money. After Bill and Marcy talk it over, the two of them choose number three.

At age 50 Bill is no longer feeling so good about his financial future.

Now Bill is 65. The financial storm of his kids' tuition is a distant memory of years gone by. He and Marcy have survived and are glad they gave their kids the gift of a good education. Yes, he did have to delay his retirement until age 65, but that, too, was a small price to pay. Each of their three children has graduated from college, and all three have good jobs. Lauren owns her own business and is able to juggle all the demands of a working mother of three. Tommy has become an attorney at a local practice in town. And Scott is a high school math teacher in a neighboring community. Bill and Marcy had borrowed what they needed to make it work and have spent most of the years since then paying off the debt they had accumulated. They were also committed to having their house paid off by the time Bill retired in order to save that expense in retirement. It is a goal they have achieved just in time. They are now debt free and ready to take on the new adventure of retirement, grandkids, and leisure.

Although Bill had not been able to continue to save money in his 401(k) after Lauren's junior year, his original contributions have grown to quite a large sum. His account now stands at a whopping $3,091,808. Bill sits back in his chair and lets out an audible sigh. *Wow, even with those tough years, I have still accumulated over three million dollars.* Bill is glad he had chosen to invest in his 401(k).

Good thing I invested as much as I could in those early years. I guess I did receive good advice.

BUT … that was before Bill began taking money *out* of his account. Two months before Bill's retirement, a new president of the United States had been elected. Along with a new president, the country also elected a new Congress and Senate. All three had the same agenda – begin to pay down the horrific national debt. The country was now serious about attacking the problem and had elected a government it believed would save them from the devastating nightmare of insurmountable debt. The future of America was at stake.

What Americans didn't understand and what was never spoken of during the months of campaigning was *how* this administration was going to accomplish this task. Those running for office had talked about cutting programs and eliminating governmental waste; the country bought it hook, line, and sinker. No true American wanted to see their country go under, and many believed it was now or never to salvage the mess. However, along with those original campaign promises lurked the real method of accomplishing the task, which was to raise taxes.

Although taxes had continued to go up over the last 15 years, this new tax increase was the granddaddy of them all. Bill's federal tax rate had risen to 55% overnight. He was stunned. To make matters worse, he no longer had any deductions to offset his retirement income. His kids are grown and his house is paid off. All the deductions he used when he was younger have now evaporated. Every dollar he takes out of his 401(k) is going to be taxed – and taxed hard.

Wait a minute! Bill thinks. *What happened to lower tax rates in retirement because my income is lower? What happened to the idea of saving the tax during the contribution phase because it is better in the long run?*

Bill quickly realizes that the few thousand dollars he had

postponed in taxes when he was young will now likely cost him well over a million dollars. For the first time it dawns on him that he had never really *avoided* taxes; he had simply *delayed* them. And by delaying them Bill has only compounded them, making them far, far worse than he could have ever imagined. Worse than *anyone* could have imagined.

At age 65 Bill is feeling a little sick to his stomach. Uncle Sam is going to ruin his golden years.

It is now five years since Bill's death. He passed away at the age of 80, and Marcy survived her husband by four additional years. It has been nearly a year since she went to rest beside her husband. All three kids appreciated the financial sacrifices of their parents. For over a year they have worked hard at settling all the estate issues. It has been extremely complicated and far more time consuming than any of the three had ever imagined.

But the biggest shock of all arrived when they got the final distribution from their parents' 401(k).

In Bill's later years he had confided in his kids about how much money he had saved. He preserved his original savings of $3,091,808 because he didn't know how long Marcy or he might live, and he didn't want to run out of money while one of them was still living. He knew if he began to spend down his account, he might end up with nothing left to sustain Marcy in her later years if he predeceased her, which was a likely event. He didn't want to take that risk. In order to do this, they lived frugally. With the new tax rates, Bill and Marcy had only been able to live a shadow of the life they were accustomed to. (He never shared *this* part of his retirement with his kids.)

Once Bill and Marcy's estate was settled and the 401(k) funds were distributed, the kids thought there must certainly be some mistake. Of the nearly three million in their father's account, only

$476,368 (or 15%) was passed on to them. Instead of each child receiving close to $1,000,000, after taxes the three children ended up with just over $150,000 each. Although Scott is nearly retired from teaching math, he knows his skills aren't that rusty. Something has to be in error. He calls a local accountant to show him the situation. After careful review the CPA tells him that, indeed, the numbers are correct. With the newly instated federal, state, and estate tax rates imposed by Congress, taxes have taken a full 85% of his father's qualified retirement account.

The kids are shocked. Why hadn't someone warned their father about this situation? Why hadn't someone warned *them* about this situation? Why hadn't someone showed their father a better way to save for his future?

As they asked around to other financial professionals in the community, they quickly realized the answer ... no one they talked to *knew* of a better way.

Although Bill has long since passed, had he realized what Uncle Sam was going to take from his savings once he and Marcy were gone, he would have said to himself, *I definitely don't feel good about my financial past or my kids' financial future.*

For some of you, this fictitious story may have many similarities to your own life. For others, this may look nothing like your reality; that is always the danger of using examples. You may be older or younger, female not male, make more money or less money. You may be a business owner and have never worked for a corporation a day in your life. Or you might have worked for multiple companies in your career (and probably have). You might not have a matching provision for your 401(k). As a matter of fact, you might not even have a 401(k) – but that's okay! Whatever your situation may be, you could face the same potentially devastating tax disaster unless you choose a better way!

In this book I will show you there *is* a better way to save money for your future. A simple way. A way that, based on current tax laws as of this writing, won't make you feel like your money is being held captive until retirement age. A way that allows you to get at your retirement savings at *any age* without paying tax on the gain (if utilized properly*) ... that's right ... *zero!* A way that does not hold you hostage to the changing tax rates of the future. And a way that gives you a better chance of living a fully-funded retirement, enjoying all the things you want to do, while still leaving behind a potentially huge legacy that will pass to the next generation, free from federal and state income taxes.

* Please consult a licensed and trained insurance professional in your specific state in order to fully understand how to properly utilize this strategy. This book is not intended to sell or recommend any product. Nor is it intended to fully educate you on the strategy. It is simply intended to introduce you to a concept you may not currently be familiar with. The only way to find out what is best suited to your specific needs is to consult a licensed insurance agent in your local area who understands this concept.

Chapter 13

Retirement Trap #1 – The Tax Trap

Remember, Bill's story may be nothing like your own. You may be single, or you may be married with no kids. You may make $30,000 a year, or you may make $300,000 a year. You may be a corporate executive, or you may run a small business out of your home. It really doesn't matter. What does matter is that you understand all of the issues at play in this story because they could affect *you* in a similar manner.

In these next four chapters, I'd like to explore the dangers that lie beneath the surface of the obvious. Dangers that could potentially destroy the financial golden years of your life. Dangers that I have named the *Retirement Traps*.

To begin let's look at the make-up of most people's retirement accounts once they reach retirement age. Do you think most of their accumulated savings are contribution or gain? If you said gain you'd be correct ... by a wide margin.

Let's look at some real numbers to see just how significant this really is. If someone were to contribute only $100 a month into a retirement account over a 30-year period, that person would have contributed $36,000. If that amount grew by 7% a year for 30 years, that $36,000 would have grown into a whopping $121,997 – a 239% total return!

If this individual had been contributing to a tax-qualified retirement plan, they would have delayed (not saved) the tax on their $36,000 contribution. Generally speaking, an individual's net taxable income will be lowest in the early years of their career, not just because they are earning less but also because they typically have the most tax deductions – the two major ones being mortgage interest and children in the home. So even if someone is a fairly high-income earner, their *net* tax rate might end up being as low as 18-20% due to itemized write-offs.

So let's calculate the current tax delay (not savings) for the individual who has contributed $36,000, using a 20% net tax rate just to be conservative. Twenty percent of $36,000 is a total tax deferral (not savings) of $7,200 during all of those 30 years of accumulation.

Well now, that's not bad. We would all like to save $7,200. But let's not forget that tax was never saved; it was just delayed.

As I mentioned previously, if we apply a 7% annual growth rate to the total contribution, this individual would end up with around $121,997 in their retirement account. Although we don't know what tax rate this individual might expect to pay at retirement (we will address this later), we can guess they likely have lost some of their previous tax deductions.

A primary goal for many retirees is to own their home debt-free. They don't want a mortgage payment chipping away at their retirement income. Therefore, many retired people no longer have the benefit of a mortgage deduction on their income tax. At the same time, since their children are grown and have moved out (hopefully), they also do not have the benefit of claiming their children as dependents. The net effect? Fewer tax deductions. And fewer tax deductions translate into a higher *net* tax rate.

Before we look at the probable tax scenario this individual will face in retirement, we need to make an assumption; we need to guess what this individual's *net* tax rate will be in retirement. For simplicity, let's be very generous and assume the same low net tax rate of only 20% in retirement. If we apply that rate to the total balance of the tax-qualified plan, you get a whopping tax liability of $24,399. Ouch! That doesn't sound very appealing. So much for the benefits of the $7,200 tax deferral. That deferral just cost the individual nearly three-and-a-half times more in actual taxes to be paid over the lifetime of withdrawals from their account. And the death-tax picture is even worse.

The reality, however, is that the net tax rate in retirement could be higher than the net tax during the accumulation years, even if this individual's gross income is exactly the same or even less. Again, this could be due to the loss of some key tax deductions that were available to them in their earlier years. In reality, this individual's net tax rate could easily be 30% to 40%, especially if they live in a state with a moderately high state income tax. If the net tax rate was 30%, the total tax liability would be $36,599 instead of $24,399. At 40% the tax liability jumps to $48,799.

Would any of us really trade $24,399, $36,599, or $48,799 for just a *delay* of paying a small $7,200? No. Of course not! But, unfortunately, that is what millions of Americans are doing every day as they contribute to their tax-qualified plans. And remember, these numbers are based on a small savings of only $100 per month. If a person were to save $1,000 per month, as allowed by most tax-qualified plans, then the problem would become *ten times* worse. That appealing deduction on taxes today might end up costing $243,990, $365,990, $487,990, or more.

What people fail to realize is that *tax-qualified plans do not avoid tax, they simply delay tax. And by delaying tax these plans compound tax, making the tax burden worse – much, much worse.*

Step back for a minute and ask yourself, "Whose retirement am I planning?" Is there any question why the government promotes tax-qualified programs? Uncle Sam is building *his* retirement at *your* expense.

In Chapter 19 I am going to show you how this individual, in the previously discussed scenario, can pay the $7,200 tax on their contribution today but then be able to access the $121,997 *tax-free.* Not just tax-delayed – tax-free.

As we look at the next issue regarding taxation, let me ask you a critical question. Do you believe future taxes will be higher or lower than they are today? Think about this for a moment. Over the years I have asked this question frequently to get a gauge of the public's opinion on future taxation. And guess what? Every person, without fail, has told me they expected higher tax rates in the future. Every one. And I fully agree.

Think about what we are facing as a country. We have undertaken a long and costly war on terrorism. Who's going to pay that bill? Supposedly, we are building a wall on our southern border. Who's going to pay that bill? (Not Mexico, I assure you.) We have a public-sector employee pension fund shortage to the tune of about $4 trillion.[viii] And still I ask the question, who's going to pay that bill?

The answer to all three questions is … you. You the American taxpayer. Please know, I am not editorializing on any of the above items. You may be one who agrees with these expenditures or you may be one who disagrees with them. It really doesn't matter. You are still going to pay the bill. And while these are some large and immediate expenses that will affect the economy and the national budget for years to come, I believe there are three even more daunting issues, lingering on the horizon, that must be addressed to prevent a potential, national, financial collapse.

The first of these issues is our failing Social Security system. Soon there will be one worker supporting every retired person. And don't think for a second that your Social Security contributions are sitting in a nice little account for you to access someday. They're not. No, they are already spent. Every penny of them. It's a pay-as-you-go system that is on the brink of disaster. Back in 2007, when the first edition of *Tax-Free Retirement*™ was published, the front page of every Social Security statement had these words,

"About Social Security's future...

"For more than 60 years, America has kept the promise of security for its workers and their families. But now, the Social Security system is facing serious future financial problems, and action is needed soon to make sure that the system is sound when today's younger workers are ready for retirement.

*"Today, there are almost 36 million Americans age 65 or older. Their Social Security retirement benefits are funded by today's workers and their employers who jointly pay Social Security taxes – just as the money they paid into Social Security was used to pay benefits to those who retired before them. **Unless action is taken soon to strengthen Social Security, in just 14 years [2021] we will begin paying more in benefits than we collect in taxes. Without changes, by 2042 the Social Security Trust Fund will be exhausted.** By then the number of Americans*

65 or older is expected to have doubled. There won't be enough younger people working to pay all of the benefits owed to those who are retiring. At that point, there will be enough money to pay only about 73 cents for each dollar of scheduled benefits."[ix]

Why do you think the government printed these words on the front page of the Social Security statement and began sending them out to every worker, every year? Is it because they know of the coming disaster and want to cover their own backsides? Although most Americans don't read these statements and do not know this pending disaster even exists, the government wants the liability to be back on us as individuals so no one can ever say, "No one ever told me I wasn't going to have a Social Security benefit!" All the government has to say is, "We told you so, every year, for the last 30 years. Don't blame us!"

In 2010, just three years after the previous statement, the verbiage had been revised to:

"Currently, the Social Security Board of Trustees projects program costs to rise by 2035 so that taxes will be enough to pay for only 75 percent of scheduled benefits. This increase in cost results from population aging, not because we are living longer, but because birth rates dropped from three to two children per woman. Importantly, this shortfall is basically stable after 2035; adjustments to taxes or benefits that offset the effects of the lower birth rate may restore solvency for the Social Security program on a sustainable basis for the foreseeable future. Finally, as Treasury debt securities (trust fund assets) are redeemed in the future, they will just be replaced with public debt. If trust fund assets are exhausted without reform, benefits will necessarily be lowered with no effect on budget deficits."[x]

Do you see what happened? In those three short years, the Social Security Administration reduced the predicted time to get to roughly 75% of scheduled benefits by seven years, from 2042 to 2035. You see, the Social Security solvency train is careening down the backside of a mountain pass without any brakes, and it's headed for derailment. And that's not just some wild speculation. That's a prediction straight from the pages of the Social Security website itself.

On January 11, 2005, President George W. Bush made the following remarks at Andrew W. Mellon Auditorium in Washington, D.C. "Now, I readily concede some would say, well, it's [Social Security] not bankrupt yet; why don't we wait until it's bankrupt? The problem with that notion is that the longer you wait, the more difficult it is to fix. You realize that this system of ours is going to be short the difference between obligation and money coming in, by about $11 trillion, unless we act. And that's an issue. That's trillion with a 'T.'"

And that was in 2005.

What? An eleven TRILLION-dollar shortfall in 2005 just for Social Security? How can that be possible? That's 139% of the total *published* national debt in that same year.[xi]

On January 13, 2005, Vice President Cheney echoed the president's remarks in a speech at Catholic University. "Again, the projected shortfall in Social Security exceeds $10 trillion; that figure is nearly twice the combined wages and salaries of every single working American last year."

Whoa!

I chose to retain the statements by former President Bush and former Vice President Cheney from my first edition of this book to show what was being predicted, at the highest level of government, twelve years ago.

And as you might have guessed, Social Security has continued its rapid decline. The current predictions by the Congressional Budget Office, which provides a Nonpartisan Analysis for the U.S. Congress, are, *"Under current law, CBO projects, Social Security's trust funds, considered together, will be exhausted in 2029. In that case, benefits in 2030 would need to be reduced by 29 percent from the scheduled amounts."*[xii]

Once again, we see another six years chopped off the prediction of when Social Security will face its day of reckoning. But not only has the time frame been reduced once again, the benefit amount has been reduced, as well, from 75% to 71% of scheduled benefits – a further 4% decline from the SSA's prediction in 2010.

In reality, I don't believe the government will let Social Security fail, because it would have a public uprising on its hands unlike anything America has seen in recent years; but to keep the program viable, it has only one option – higher taxes!

The second issue that I believe will cause us to face much higher taxation in the future is our country's immense national debt. It has spiraled out of control and now stands at an unimaginable $19,844,971,925 (almost $20 trillion), as of July 2017, according to truthinaccounting.org.[xiii] That means we have increased our debt by over $11 trillion in the last 11 years (It is now 232% of the $8.5 trillion debt in October 2006). This is an average increase to our national debt of $2.7 billion *per day*, every single day, since my first edition was released. This shows that not only is the amount of our total national debt rapidly increasing but the *pace* of its increase is rising as well. Back in October 2006, the average daily increase was $1.6 billion. Today's $2.7 billion daily increase means we are now adding to our debt 168% faster than in 2006.

That, however, is just the *published* national debt. The debt we've already incurred as a nation. Unfortunately, the reality is far worse.

Our *real* national debt, as would be accounted for by any other entity except the Federal Government (including corporations and state governments), is a knee-weakening $102 trillion or $128 trillion according to truthinaccounting.org and usdebtclock.org, respectively. That's between five and six times greater than the current published debt. What's the difference between the *published* debt and the real debt? A lot. While the *published* debt represents the dollars we have already spent, the *real* debt takes into account all of our assets and liabilities, as reported in the Financial Report of the US Government, as well as our unfunded Social Security and Medicare promises.[xiv] It is a far more accurate picture of the debt we are really facing as a nation. But let me bring this even closer to home. In order for us to pay off our *real* national debt, as it stands currently, every U.S. taxpayer would have to contribute $985,624.[xv] Think about that! That's just your share based on our *current* shortfall. It doesn't even take into account any future budget additions.

With it growing at an unprecedented rate, this mammoth mountain may already be insurmountable. At some point, however, it will need to be addressed. And there are only two ways to address this problem. Spend less or collect more. Do you hear what I hear? Higher taxes!

I believe it is more clear than ever that the only way we are going to survive financially as a nation will be by significantly increasing taxes on everyone in the years and decades to come; the bills need to be paid because the alternative is unspeakable.

The third issue that I believe will cause higher tax rates in the future is the ongoing inferno of the health care system in America. The costs are out of control, as individuals are living longer and demanding more services and more prescription drugs than ever before. Lump on top of that the lack of litigation control, and you have a recipe for true disaster.

Ten years ago I wrote, *"It is my personal opinion, as well as the view of many of my friends in the health care industry, that the eventual result in America will be similar to that in other developed countries – a government-run health care program. The funding vehicle, once again, will have to be higher taxes for Americans!"*[xvi]

And we saw the first step in that direction on March 23, 2010, when President Obama signed into law The Patient Protection and Affordable Care Act, soon nicknamed Obamacare.

Who knows if the government will eventually take over the entire health care system? But even if they don't, think what is happening to our population. It is aging rapidly. Baby boomers are reaching retirement age in record numbers. And what health care plan are *all* American citizens on at the age of 65? Medicare. *Tax-funded health care!* In other words we are going to have an increasing number of individuals on government-sponsored health care, one way or another. People will continue to live longer which will result in the need for more medical care at older ages. This will be further exacerbated by the increasing availability and life-prolonging effects of new prescription drug technology, again adding even more years to our already increasing life spans. And as you can guess, there is only one logical way to pay for this increased demand for medical care services by a growing, elderly population – higher taxes!

Although this is merely a cursory list of the issues we face which could drive up taxes in the future, one thing I believe is true. Americans will be faced with much higher tax rates in the decades ahead.

So, if this is indeed the case, would you rather pay your taxes now or later? Not only can you pay tax on a much smaller *amount* now, but you might likely do so at potentially lower tax *rates* as well, thus compounding your savings effect. The other option is to have your entire nest egg taxed at potentially astronomical rates in the future.

Chapter 14

Retirement Trap #2 – The Access Trap

Why do you think most Americans plan to retire around the age of 60 or 65? Is it a coincidence that these ages coincide with the years in which the individual has access to either their tax-qualified retirement plans or their Social Security benefits?

As a bit of an aside, I believe the entire concept of retirement has been spoon-fed to the American public by the government and financial planners for so long that few individuals ever stop to ask a few basic questions. Why do I want to retire? If I do plan to retire, why am I choosing the age at which I will do so? What am I going to spend the rest of my life doing?

A friend of mine who retired a number of years ago, after serving as a corporate executive for decades, shared with me some interesting insights. He said, "Patrick, people did a great job of helping me set up my finances for retirement. Actually, it was quite simple. No one, however, helped me prepare my *life* for this next season. I knew this date was coming for years, but I never really spent time thinking about what I would do, how I would spend my time, or what I would pursue next."

I believe a lot of people have set a retirement date in the future simply because ... because 59 ½ is when they can access their tax-qualified retirement account ... because 65 is when they will receive their full social security benefits ... because, because, because, because, because ... sounds like a song from *The Wizard of Oz.*

I would like to see people separate their desired date for retirement from simply the date in which they are able to access their money. The strategy I am going to show you will do this. Fully. Completely. But for now let's explore *Trap #2 – The Access Trap.*

Remember our friend Bill? How much did it cost him to access money from his 401(k) to help fund his daughter's college education? Since Bill was still working and earning a good income, all money pulled out of his retirement plan had to be added to his existing income, sending him into the highest marginal tax bracket very quickly. We assumed his federal tax bracket was 40% - essentially the same as today's top rate in 2017. He also had a 10% state tax and a 10% early withdrawal tax penalty. Therefore, Bill had to fork over 60 cents of every dollar to the IRS in order to pull money out of his retirement account before age 59½. Sixty cents!

So in order to fund just one year of his daughter's $90,000 tuition bill (which, unfortunately, is likely what a year of private school tuition could cost 14 years from now at 6% annual tuition increase), Bill would have had to withdraw $225,000 in actual dollars and then cough up $135,000 of that to Uncle Sam. Who in their right mind would do that? No one.

Can you see why Bill was frustrated? Can you see why he felt his money was being held hostage? I certainly would feel that way, and I'm sure you would too.

In basic terms *The Access Trap* is simple. Your money is not really your own, at least not until you meet the government's eligibility guidelines as to when you can access your money within a tax-qualified plan. But don't forget that even when you are able to access your tax-qualified funds and avoid the 10% early withdrawal tax *penalty*, you are *still* crushed by the federal and state income taxes that are due.

When you step back and see this reality in black and white, it really does sound a bit criminal, doesn't it?

One of the questions people ask me when they hear about this new retirement concept is, "Why isn't everyone doing this?"

I look back at them and say, "The only reason I can think of why everyone isn't taking advantage of this strategy is because most people have never heard about this concept before. Think about yourself. Before today, had you ever heard about this idea?"

"No," they reply.

"Well," I continue, "Everyone else is just like you. Quite frankly, I have been working in this industry for 25 years, and in my experience very few of my colleagues in the financial world fully understand the incredible benefits of this strategy themselves."

It was my desire that the first edition of *Tax-Free Retirement*™ would bridge this gap that has held the public back from the most advantageous wealth accumulation and distribution tool that, in my opinion, has ever existed. And I believe it did that. I'm hopeful that this second edition will do even more to minimize that gap in understanding and education.

As we conclude this chapter, let me leave you with some final questions to ponder about *The Access Trap*. Do you really want to sock all of your long-term savings away into an account that can't be touched without paying penalties and taxes? Wouldn't it be better if you had full access to your money at *any time* and at *any age*? Might you adjust your retirement plans if that were the case? Maybe you would work your current job until the age of 50 and then pursue one of your life-long dreams. Would you write that book you've always wanted to write? Would you start that business you've always pondered? Would you take up flying lessons, travel, work part-time, or volunteer in your community?

If you had access to your retirement savings at any age, you would be freed up to take a step backward in earned income. Slow down. Take a break. Take a sabbatical. Work three days a week. Pursue your dreams. Enjoy your kids. Dote on your grandkids. You name it because it would be *your* choice. And these choices would be available to you at any age, assuming you had saved enough money to provide an adequate income for yourself and your family.

You might find you love your new occupation so much that you never plan to retire because you are finally pursuing your life's dream. You are energized. You're full of life. More life than you have ever experienced.

And if you find you love your new occupation so much that you plan to keep working well into your twilight years, and it is providing the necessary income to meet your living expenses, you could let the savings in your nest egg continue to grow indefinitely. If you utilize the strategies I'm going to show you in the coming chapters, there is no age in which you are forced to begin taking income. You can let your nest egg grow and accumulate for some exciting future possibilities.

But this is *not* the case with tax-qualified retirement plans. There is not only a *Tax Trap* and an *Access Trap*, but there is also a *Distribution Trap*. Let's explore.

Chapter 15

Retirement Trap #3 – The Distribution Trap

This is going to be a short chapter because *The Distribution Trap* is relatively simple to understand. Yes, there are many laws and rules that determine how it actually plays out for the individual, but I often find that less is more.

All you need to know about *The Distribution Trap* is how it works and how it can affect your future.

In simple terms the IRS wants to get *its* hands on *its* retirement. Sure, the account may have your name on it, but when 30, 40, or even 50 percent of your distribution can go to the bureaucratic coffers, you have to step back and wonder, "Whose retirement is this anyway?"

Here's how it works. By April 1st the year after you reach the age of 70½, you *must* begin taking a distribution from your tax-qualified retirement account, whether that is a 401(k), a Traditional IRA, a SEP, a SIMPLE, or any other type of qualified retirement plan. The government provides guidelines on how much this distribution must be each year, and it varies by a number of different factors. There are many free web sites that provide calculators for individuals to estimate the amount that is required to be withdrawn; however … not to worry. The company that manages your plan is responsible for notifying you as to the amount which you are required to take.

So what happens if you don't take this mandatory distribution? Well, I'd like for you to read it straight from IRS Publication 590.[xvii] (This is referring specifically to a traditional IRA, but by the time an individual is 70½, that's most likely where their money will be. I'll explain why after we look at the quote from the IRS publication.) It reads:

> "You cannot keep amounts in your traditional IRA indefinitely. Generally, you must begin receiving distributions by April 1 of the year following the year in which you reach age 70 ½. The required minimum distribution for any year after the year in which you reach age 70 ½ must be made by December 31 of that later year.
>
> *Tax on excess.* If distributions are less than the required minimum distribution for the year, discussed earlier under *When Must You Withdraw Assets? (Required Minimum Distributions)*, you may have to pay a 50% excise tax for that year on the amount not distributed as required."

The reason this rule affects just about everyone is because once a person retires, they often have to (and generally choose to) roll their tax-qualified money into a new, self-directed Traditional IRA. Why? Because they are no longer officially associated with their prior company of employment, and either the company won't allow them to continue with their tax-qualified plan, or they choose to place their money in a plan that allows them to control the financial decisions themselves. But even if they are one of the few individuals who can keep their money in their existing plan and choose to do so, it really doesn't make a difference because the *laws of distribution for other tax-qualified plans are the same as they are for the IRA.*

So how do you feel about that excerpt from the IRS? Fifty percent excise tax! "That's got to be a joke," you say. Unfortunately, it's not. *They* are serious about getting *their* money.

So the looming question is, "If you don't need the money, do you still need to take the distribution?"

The answer is an unequivocal and resounding, "Yes!"

So let's review what we know about tax-qualified retirement plans so far.

Is most retirement money in tax-qualified plans? Yes, to the tune of *trillions* of dollars.

Can I get my money out of my plan before age 59½? Yes but not without a significant penalty and taxation. Under some special circumstances you can avoid this penalty, but for all intents and purposes you cannot.

What happens if I take money out of my plan before age 59½? On top of the substantial tax you will pay, you will also incur an additional 10% penalty.

Can I get money out of my plan tax-free after the age of 59½? Sorry. No again. Every penny in your tax-qualified account (including your original contributions) will be taxed at your current tax bracket at the *time of withdrawal.*

What if I don't need the money in retirement? ***Can I let it accrue in my plan and pass it along to my heirs***? Once again, no. Regardless of whether you need the money or not, you must begin withdrawing it in the year after you reach age 70½.

What about at death? How does this plan get taxed? Glad you asked. That's Retirement Trap #4 – *The Death Trap.* If you thought the other three traps were bad, just wait until you understand this one.

Chapter 16

Retirement Trap #4 – The Death Trap

The Titanic was a great ship. It was the grandest the world had ever seen. It had just one small problem – it didn't make it to its destination. With all its lavish décor and advanced engineering, it couldn't do what even the relatively primitive sailing ships of Columbus had done more than 400 years before.

Why? Why didn't the Titanic make it to its destination? The answer is simple – it hit an iceberg.

Have you ever thought about what would happen if you hit an iceberg? Not literally, like the Titanic, but figuratively. You see, the Titanic's experience is not too different from that of our own everyday lives. We have icebergs lurking in our waters. Financial icebergs. Sickness icebergs. Accident icebergs. Catastrophe icebergs. Each one eager to sink and destroy. Eager to send us plummeting into the depths, broken and tattered. Eager to keep us from our destination.

For those of you participating in tax-qualified retirement plans, have you ever thought about what would happen if you hit the granddaddy of all icebergs – the Death Iceberg? What if you hit it tomorrow? What if you hit it in ten years? Maybe you won't hit it until a ripe old age. But know one thing; this is an iceberg you *will* hit. And when you do, what will be left behind for those you love and who love you?

So how does death affect the results of tax-qualified retirement plans? Let's take a look.

Death can present itself in two forms – expected and unexpected. During our lifetimes we have all probably experienced both. The phone call out of the blue telling us what we least want to hear. There's been an accident – unexpected.

And likely, we have sat by the bedside of someone who slowly slipped away from us, after a long life of loving, warm memories – expected.

Eventually, each of us will fall into one of those two categories – expected or unexpected – and when we do, *all* the decisions we have made during our life will leave ripples in the waters of those left behind.

Let's look at just one of those decisions. The decision to use a tax-qualified retirement plan.

Iceberg #1 – Premature Death

When people sit down with their financial planners or their companies' plan administrators to talk about retirement planning, what picture do you think they have in mind?

I can tell you because I sit with these same people every day. They picture themselves, at some golden age in the distant future, on the golf course, sipping Mai Tais in Maui, traveling the world, visiting their grandkids, serving their community. Something. Anything. What they don't picture is dying tomorrow.

Their picture of the future extends way beyond tomorrow. Quite frankly, it usually extends way beyond the next decade. Most individuals don't stop long enough to ask the all-important question, "What if my future is only tomorrow?"

That is the question that none of us likes to face. We somehow feel it is too morbid. So what do we do instead? We ignore it. We pretend the reality of premature death doesn't exist. And as we go through life pretending this reality doesn't exist, we make decisions that could rip apart the lives of those we love and leave behind.

Would it have been too morbid for the engineers of the Titanic to ask a similar question, "What happens if this ship hits an iceberg?"

Of course not. Not only was this *not* a morbid question, it was a critically important question, as they unfortunately came to find out. It's simply called planning.

The reason I have spent so much time laying this foundation is because the lack of planning for premature death has led many people to make a common and critical financial error. They don't leave enough money for those left behind.

This lack of money can occur in one of two ways. First, because an individual's savings has not had the power of compound interest or time, it can be a fraction of their eventual nest egg. For example, if a person were able to put $1,000 per month into their tax-qualified plan, they could possibly expect to build a nest egg north of $1,000,000 in thirty years, a reasonable saving period for a working individual. And it's that number that sticks in their brain. It's that number that fuels their retirement dreams.

But what if all of that is stopped short? What if they hit an iceberg? What if they make one monthly deposit into their plan and then find themselves the victim of premature death? Their account stands at the value of their deposit – a whopping total of $1,000. Even if the unexpected didn't happen for five years, their account would still sit at a number far less than $100,000 – hardly enough to fund a family's needs or a spouse's future.

Second, the other way this lack of money can occur is by not having enough life insurance. In my 25 years in the insurance industry, I have *never – not even once –* met with an individual who has had adequate life insurance in place prior to our meeting. Think about that for a moment. I have met with hundreds of people, and not once has a person actually had a sufficient amount of death benefit. That example, by itself, should be enough proof that people don't like to face the reality of premature death.

I'm sure there are many reasons why people leave too little money for those left behind, but I believe they ultimately boil down to the same two reasons we have already discussed: No. 1 – People don't think they will die prematurely, and, No. 2 – People greatly underestimate how much money it will really take to provide for the loved ones they leave behind.

Throughout my career my calculations have generally shown it takes somewhere between seven to ten times an annual income, in liquid cash, to properly protect a family. Since most people aren't able to stash away that amount of money in a bank or investment account, that leaves the bulk of the burden to rest on the shoulders of life insurance.

But how much life insurance do people actually have? My experience shows that most have somewhere between one to three times their incomes. A sizeable shortage, to say the least.

Before I leave you completely discouraged, I want to give you the good news. Don't despair. Take hope. In the next chapter I am going to give you the solution that will render the iceberg of premature death obsolete, at least in regard to your finances and the future of your loved ones. If you follow this strategy, you may be able to remove this iceberg from your personal financial waters. But before you skip ahead to the solution, please read the next section *carefully* because there is an equally daunting iceberg that still lurks below the water line, waiting to put a hole in your financial ship. Keep going. You're almost there.

Iceberg #2 – Expected Death

Hopefully you will find yourself in the majority of the population and experience a wonderfully long life. Hopefully, your golden years will be full and rewarding.

If that is the case, then all your planning and saving will have been a worthy undertaking that will fuel the dreams you pondered so long. It will be time to enjoy the fruits of your labor.

However, I do not think the proper vision of retirement is one of lethargy and laziness, a time to stop working; rather, a great vision of retirement is one for increased investment – maybe not financial but certainly relational. A time for increased investment in your spouse, if you have one. Or your children or grandchildren. A time to share your wisdom with the next generation. A time to volunteer at civic organizations that desperately need assistance. Yes, retirement can be the richest of all seasons in life. No wonder it is called the Golden Years.

However, all of these relational investments take time, and as the old adage goes, time is money. If you have saved diligently for retirement, then you have accrued a sum of money to help pay the bills. Hopefully you have saved enough to pay *all* of the bills.

However, one interesting fact I have found to be true with good savers is they tend to remain good savers in retirement. This may sound hard to believe, but for some it is incredibly difficult to begin *spending* the money that they have been accumulating for so long. To become a consumer of their retirement monies requires a drastic change in their thinking. And many people don't make the switch easily.

Another issue retirees face is the fact that their savings have to last for their entire lifetimes. The difficulty of that proposition is that no one knows how long they are going to live. People figure out very quickly that, when they do start spending their retirement money, they need to be careful and conserve it so it will last longer than they do.

One method of stretching money out I have frequently seen practiced is for retirees to spend only the growth (or interest) in their account, leaving their original nest egg intact. This gives them comfort and provides the security they desire. For some, this will provide enough income to live their dreams, but for most, it won't. But, regardless, because people want to preserve their nest egg, there is generally money left in the account at the retiree's death. Often *lots* of money!

Please note my next statement, because it is one of the most important statements I will make in this book. ***In my opinion the single worst place to have money at death is in a tax-qualified account.***

Why? What happens to money left in a tax-qualified plan at the time of death? Let me tell you. It's not pretty. As a matter of fact, it's downright ugly.

Tax-qualified plans get treated differently, depending on whether or not the money is passing to a living spouse. If the retiree is married, the account will pass on to the spouse with no taxation issues. However, if the retiree is not married or has been predeceased by his or her spouse, the account gets absolutely obliterated by taxes. Likewise, if the tax-qualified plan is passed on to a living spouse, the account will get similarly devastated at the death of that spouse. So there is no escape. Let me describe the pending disaster.

As you are likely aware, federal tax rates are broken into different percentages based on varying income brackets. In 2017 the federal income tax brackets look like this:[xviii]

SINGLE	MARRIED-JOINT RETURN	HEAD OF HOUSEHOLD	MARGINAL TAX RATE
$0	$0	$0	10%
$9,326	$18,651	$13,351	15%
$37,951	$75,901	$50,801	25%
$91,901	$153,101	$131,201	28%
$191,651	$233,351	$212,501	33%
$416,701	$416,701	$416,701	35%
$418,401+	$470,701+	$444,551+	39.6%

When you are talking about a person's life savings, it really doesn't take much of a contribution over a 30- or 40-year period to accumulate an account worth more than $400,000.

So please read these next words very carefully! *If you pass your tax-qualified account to heirs upon your death (except if passing to a spouse),* **that money gets treated as taxable income earned in that year, by the receiving heir, and gets taxed at the appropriate tax rate.** Do you see what that means? Can you tell how that would impact the value of your account?

Let's put some numbers to this. It is not uncommon to see $1,000,000 or more left in a tax-qualified plan at the participant's death. Remember, most retirees don't want to spend down the principal in their account because they don't want the money to run out before they die.

At today's top tax rate, a $1,000,000 tax-qualified account passed on to the next generation at an individual's death would get hit with $341,231 in federal income tax and $90,000 in state income tax (if you live in a state with a 9% income tax). That's a whopping $431,231 vaporized immediately. And not to beat a dead horse, but if marginal tax rates rise (which I believe will be a necessity in the future), that 39.6% could go up to 50%, 55%, 60%, or higher. No one knows!

As a side note, I discuss in my book *The Retirement Miracle* that the top marginal federal tax rates back in the mid-1940s reached a peak of 94% in 1944 and 1945. So a top U.S. tax rate of 60% or higher isn't as ludicrous as it sounds. We have been there before, during a trying time in our nation's history. We could certainly get there again.

As ridiculous as that may seem to you, I think the government could sell those tax rates to the general public, quite easily, making them believe they are not affected because it would only affect the "rich." In reality, it would be the biggest scam of the century. Here's why.

Every time there is a tax debate, one of the political parties pushes to lower tax rates for the lower and middle classes while raising taxes on the wealthy. Many Americans believe that sounds reasonable. They think, "Hey, I'm not one of those 'rich' Americans, so what do I care? Stick it to 'em! They can afford to pay the taxes."

So let's say that some time in the future an administration proposes to have a top marginal tax rate of 55% but only on those who make more than $1,000,000 per year. They would show the statistics that something like .05% of Americans fall into that category, so it would affect very few individuals. The public would buy it because it wouldn't affect them. Or would it?

Indeed it would. America would be duped. It would be the con of the century. It would foster one of the largest wealth transfers in history, but the transfer would flow in one direction – right into Uncle Sam's pockets.

As we have discussed, we are approaching the largest bubble of retirees and, consequently, retirement monies in history. Many middle-class Americans will accumulate retirement savings in excess of $1,000,000. If these new tax rates were to be enacted, then instead of $431,231 being paid in taxes at death, it could be $600,000 or more. It is conceivable that 60% or more of a person's tax-qualified account could be paid in taxes upon their death. Immediately. Permanently.

An issue I'm not even beginning to address in the scope of this book is the estate tax or "death tax," as derided by opponents. Trying to predict what that might look like decades in the future is like using a slingshot to try to hit an F-18 at 40,000 feet.

Even without an estate tax, do you really want to take the chance of having Uncle Sam be a 60% heir to your retirement account? It could be more. It could be less. But what if you could cut Uncle Sam out altogether? How would that feel?

Do you see why a change in the marginal tax rates doesn't affect just the wealthy?

Would you really like to save money all of your life knowing that the *majority* stakeholder at death will be the government? If you could choose who received that money, would the first person on your list be the IRS? Certainly not. Who would you give it to? Your kids? A charity? An alma mater? Your favorite niece or nephew? When you stop to think about it, you'd give it to anybody before you gave it to the government.

If you have money in a tax-qualified plan at death, you're stuck! Uncle Sam is going to get his cut – and he can hardly wait.

As I promised, we are finally there. In this next chapter I am going to show you how you can fix this problem. I'm going to show how you can give your money *to any person or organization totally and completely income-tax free.* Uncle Sam won't see a penny, at least in income tax.

Wouldn't you much rather have your money in a place you control? A place that lets you get at your money any time you want? A place that can cost you *zero* in taxes when you take your money out – if done properly? A place you can leave the money in for as long as you want? A place in which you can direct who receives the full balance at your death? And a place from which it will pass totally income-tax free to whomever you designate upon your death? I don't know about you, but that's my kind of place.

The groundwork has been set. Let's see how you can create this kind of strategy for yourself.

PART IV: THE RETIREMENT SOLUTION

Chapter 17

The Retirement Solution - The Basic Foundation

I have found that part of the reason people often miss the very best in life is because they hold misconceptions and falsehoods closely as truth. It may be because of something a parent or teacher said, a book they read, or even a television show they watched, but somewhere along the line, they created a series of truths that become inviolable while, in fact, they are completely false.

Think of some of those things in your own life. Did a parent tell you, as a child, that if you went outside in the winter with wet hair, you'd catch a cold? You certainly believed it at the time. Do you now? More than likely. What about the idea that if you pull out a gray hair, ten more will grow back? It's quite humorous what each of us hold to be true because others simply stated it as fact. We trusted the person, so we never researched the issue ourselves. We never did our own homework. It simply became our reality, and we propagated it as truth to others, as well, without so much as even a shred of proof.

When I tell you the solution to all of the problems we have raised so far in this book, you may have a negative initial reaction. You might find the voice of some previous financial advisor or book or talk show host whispering in your ear. It's possible you might have a very strong reaction. Why do I know this? For two reasons. First of all, I had that type of reaction myself; and secondly, so have many of the people I've visited with.

When I've asked them *why* they believe what they do, they could not produce an answer. That is because they were not really sure why they believe what they do. Their usual answer has been along the line of, "I don't know. Someone told me that once." Until our visit, they had never looked into the truth or figured it out for themself. They simply heard a statement, somewhere along the line, that they have held true for years.

So what is the solution to preparing financially for retirement? *My opinion is this – the single best place to save retirement dollars is in a permanent life insurance contract.*

Did you have that reaction? Did you hear the voices? You may say, "But that can't be true!" With all the jazzed up financial products on the market, how in the world can life insurance be the best place for long-term savings and wealth accumulation? Isn't life insurance about dying?

Let me start this new journey with a simple but profound explanation of how life insurance works. This basis is the foundation upon which we will build the rest of our understanding. Pretend you are sitting across from me at my desk. Let me guide you through one of the most powerful revelations you will ever experience in the financial realm. Here we go....

In this world there are only two kinds of insurance. Yes, you will hear many different names: 10-year term, second-to-die, executive benefit life, 20-year term, 30-year term, whole life, graded premium life, decreasing term, universal life, etc., etc., etc.. Every company has its own names and its own variations. But know this; there are really only two kinds of life insurance – term and permanent.

Each of these products has four unique characteristics. As I explain these characteristics, I want you to consider an analogy. Think of term insurance like *renting* a home and permanent insurance like *buying* a home. As we go through, I think you'll find amazing similarities.

I'll start with term insurance. The first characteristic of term insurance is that it is *lower cost – initially* ... just like renting a home is cheaper than buying a home. Right?

The second characteristic of term insurance, however, is that the *premium goes up over time.* Each term policy is a little different, but at some point in time the premium *will go up,* just like rent on a home. You may have signed a five-year lease with no increase in rent, but when the lease is done, what will likely happen? Rent will go up.

The third characteristic of term insurance is that it has *no cash value.* Think about it. If you rented a home for ten years and then decided to move, how much of your rent payments would the landlord give back to you? None, except maybe a small damage deposit. All the money you paid out over the years did one thing: it provided a place for you to live.

The fourth characteristic of term insurance, and the one I consider the most significant, is that at some point in the future, even if you are still alive, the coverage *will* end. For some policies it is at age 80, 85, or 90. For many it is a specified period of time, like at the end of ten or twenty years. But regardless of how long it runs, one thing is true (at least of every term policy I have ever seen) it has a drop dead point, even if *you* are still alive.

When do people need life insurance, at least the death benefit portion? The answer is simple – when they die. And when do most individuals die? The majority die when they are much older. Therefore, these term policies often terminate right before they are most needed. Unfortunately, since most term policies get so expensive in the later years of life, most have been dropped long before they have run their course. So all that money (just like rent) has been thrown to the wind.

Now let's look at permanent insurance. The first characteristic of permanent insurance is that it has a *higher cost – initially*. Just like it is generally more expensive to buy a home than it is to rent a home.

Secondly, however, the *premium stays level*. It is designed to not go up in the later years. Think about a home mortgage. If you were to take out a traditional thirty-year fixed mortgage, how much would your payment go up during those thirty years? Zero. Your 360th payment is the same as your first, at least as far as the principal and interest are concerned. Let's look at a graph (figure 17.1) to compare how the premiums for term versus permanent life insurance might look. Let's say that line "A" is the cost of term insurance and line "B" is the cost of permanent insurance. Line "B" begins much higher than line "A," but as you can see, it remains level. At some point in the future, line "A" (term insurance) will cost more, simply from an out-of-pocket expense standpoint, than line "B" (permanent insurance), just as it would cost you more out-of-pocket twenty years down the line to rent then it would if you had purchased an equivalent home at the same time you started renting.

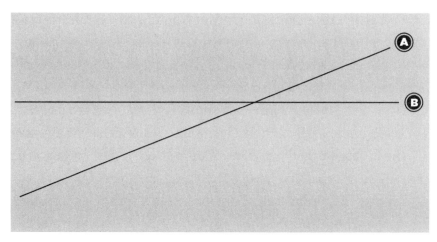

Figure 17.1

The third feature of permanent insurance is that it *builds cash value,* just like owning a home. If you lived in your home for twenty years and then sold it, you would probably get back every dollar you paid for it and likely a lot more. The same is true with permanent insurance.

The fourth and final feature of permanent insurance is that the *coverage doesn't end* as long as you continue to pay the proper premium. With most quality permanent insurance, there is not a predetermined date in the future when the coverage ceases to exist. It is designed to be there when you most need it – hopefully, much later in life.

So let's review, one last time, the four characteristics that differentiate term insurance from permanent insurance by looking at the chart below (figure 17.2):

Term Insurance	Permanent Insurance
1. Low cost — intially	1. Higher cost — intially
2. Cost goes up	2. Cost remains level
3. No cash value	3. Builds cash value
4. Coverage ends	4. Coverage never ends

Figure 17.2

With that explanation it appears I hold a strong bias toward permanent insurance, and I must tell you – I do. However, I believe both types of insurance are equally important because, just as both renting and owning a house provide a place to live, the one feature that both term and permanent insurance similarly provide is a death benefit. The most important issue in the life insurance discussion is the proper amount of death benefit coverage. If the amount of insurance needed can only be afforded through term insurance, then term it is.

However, if a person can afford the monthly (or annual) premium for permanent insurance, then just like being able to buy a home, permanent life insurance, in my opinion, is by far the preferred option.

With that simple lesson you probably now know more about life insurance than 90% of the rest of the world. Truly.

Even though the issues just discussed are significantly important in the scope of a family's financial security, I have never met a person who has actually gotten excited about figuring out the proper amount of death benefit. Many people see life insurance as a necessary evil. Many don't even see it as that. They avoid it altogether.

Here's the good news. The next few chapters should change your thinking about life insurance forever. Maybe it won't change your thinking about dealing with the death benefit portion, but you should find yourself, as silly as this may sound, thrilled about life insurance. You will see that life insurance can do far more than provide a death benefit. As a matter of fact, if structured properly, life insurance can serve as one of the most powerful retirement strategies available anywhere. I wouldn't be a bit surprised if you found yourself so excited about this new-found knowledge that you picked up the phone and set the first appointment available to get together with your insurance agent to find out what specific options may be best suited for you.

Chapter 18

The Retirement Solution – Rules of Money

When you retire you will only have two kinds of money available to you. I like to call them pots of money. The first pot of money is taxable and the second pot is tax-free. Which of the two pots would you like to have the most money in? Taxable or tax-free?

I assume you answered, "Tax-free!" But let's look at both pots of money to see how each operates.

In the taxable pot you have two different types of taxation. The first kind is called capital-gains tax. This is the tax you pay for profit on things such as stocks, mutual funds, and real estate. There are two different tax rates within the capital gains structure. One is short-term capital-gains tax, which is applied to investments held shorter than a twelve-month period; this is usually taxed at the individual's marginal income-tax rate. The second tax rate is for long-term holdings – investments held for greater than twelve months. The current (2017) capital gains tax rate on long term holdings can range between 15% and 28%, depending on what tax bracket the taxpayer is in, as well as what type of item is being sold. And of course, this is constantly subject to change based on revisions in the tax laws.

In order to illustrate this, when the first edition of this book was published in 2007, the tax on long-term holdings was only 15%. Wow! That means there has been as much as an 87% capital gains tax increase for some individuals in just the last ten years.

On the other side of the taxable pot, we have income tax – the tax you are used to paying on the income you currently earn. The types of investments that are on this side of the taxable pot consist of all forms of tax-qualified plans and any other sources of earned income. This tax can be as high as 39.6% in 2017, but as we have discussed a few times, that number could easily go up in the future and probably will.

Now let's look at the other pot of money – the tax-free pot. Although there are three common places in which to accumulate tax-free income, only two, in my opinion, are viable enough to use as retirement savings vehicles. Typically, if all the proper conditions are met, there are three accumulation vehicles available inside the tax-free pot. They are: 1) Municipal Bonds, 2) The Roth IRA,** 3) Life Insurance (if structured and managed properly – I'll elaborate later).

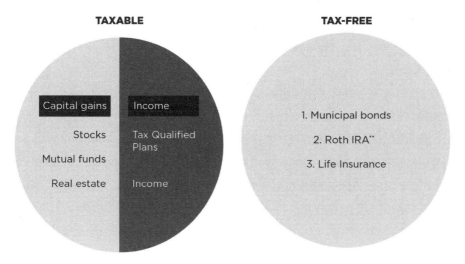

TAXABLE

Capital gains

Stocks

Mutual funds

Real estate

Income

Tax Qualified
Plans

Income

TAX-FREE

1. Municipal bonds

2. Roth IRA**

3. Life Insurance

Figure 18.1

I generally disregard number one in the tax-free pot – municipal bonds – because, over time, they have not returned enough nor provided the proper diversification to build a sufficient nest egg for retirement, in my opinion. So by eliminating number one, we are left with numbers two and three.

The Roth IRA is really a wonderful gift the government has given to us for retirement savings, but it only *begins* to do the job. Currently an individual can put only $5,500 per year into a Roth IRA ($6,500 if they are 50 or older). Although that number could eke up over the years, it is still far short of what is needed to fund an adequate retirement living, and the amount has only risen by $500 in the last 10 years. The other major disadvantage of a Roth IRA is that high-income earners can't participate. In the 2017 tax year, once a combined household income reaches $186,000, the IRS begins to phase out how much can be contributed to a Roth IRA. Once the combined household income reaches $196,000 ($133,000 for a single person), the ability to contribute is eliminated altogether.

Once again, high-income earners are treated unfairly by the government. It makes no sense. But that's the reality we have to live with.

So if your household earns more than $196,000 per year ($133,000 for an unmarried individual), you can't contribute to a Roth IRA; and since municipal bonds, in my opinion, don't provide an adequate savings venue, you are left with only one option in the tax-free pot – life insurance. Luckily, this one remaining option is a fantastic one.

Remember, which pot of money do you want filled up when you retire – the taxable one or the tax-free one? The tax-free one, of course.

Before we look at exactly how life insurance can properly provide this *Tax-Free Retirement*™ strategy, I want to share with you two *rules of money*. The first *rule of money* is a very simple, ordered list I have named *The Smart-Money Investment Order*™. It's the order in which I believe smart investment dollars should flow. I have found that, very often, people skip over the best options. I want you to be smarter than most people. (See figure 18.2)

The Smart-Money Investment Order™
1. Free Money
2. Tax-Free Money
3. Tax-Deferred Money
4. Taxable Money

Figure 18.2

Let's look quickly at each one to determine what each means and how an investor can take advantage of it.

#1 - Free Money!

Sounds great, but how do I get it? Other than gifts from family or a planned inheritance, the only place I know of in the business world where a person can receive free money is through a matching program in a 401(k) or similar plan at that individual's place of employment. "Wait a minute," you say. "The greater portion of this book has been spent explaining why employer sponsored retirement plans may *not* be the best place to save for retirement." That is true – with one exception. *Free money.* I always encourage individuals to take advantage of all the free money they can get. In other words, I encourage them to contribute (if necessary) the *minimum* amount needed to maximize the free money their company is willing to give them.

For example, let's say your company matches your contribution up to 3% of your income. If you make $60,000 per year, then you would want to contribute $1,800 ($60,000 X .03) to your employer sponsored plan because your $1,800 contribution would earn you another $1,800 match from your employer. This is free money! Take all of it you can get, as this is a 100% immediate return! However, once you reach that free money threshold, I encourage you to pause and evaluate your next best step.

Each plan is different, so check with your plan administrator to find out how much you need to contribute to maximize the free money. But once that level is reached (and it is usually quite small), if you want to follow *The Smart Money Investment Order*™, you'll want to stop because if you continue to contribute above the match amount you will have skipped over the second item on the list (Tax-Free Money) and find yourself at number three (Tax-Deferred Money).

#2 – Tax-Free Money

The "pots of money" illustration on page 121 portrays the different options you have in order to accumulate tax-free dollars. If, however, your household brings in a hefty income, you won't be able to contribute to a Roth IRA. Since muni-bonds fall short, in my opinion, I think you are left with really only one viable option – life insurance. The nice thing about life insurance, fortunately, is that it can be structured to work in a similar way to a Roth IRA but without the income limitations. Now, please note, it is **not** a Roth IRA. It is life insurance. It can simply perform in some similar manners, as I will describe in the next chapter.

But if your income threshold does allow you to contribute to a Roth IRA, that too is a very good option. It's at least a potential starting place. "But," you may ask, "If life insurance can do similar things, should I even open a Roth IRA?" The answer to that question is very individualized; it may be "yes;" it may be "no."

The first scenario I want to discuss is one in which an individual has no need for life insurance and is going to save less than the $5,500 ($6,500 if 50 or older) per year as currently allowed by a Roth IRA. If these are both true, then likely a Roth IRA *is* preferable to life insurance because the Roth IRA has no internal death-benefit cost associated with it, so every dollar that gets deposited goes directly into the investment portion (minus company fees of course).

The second scenario in which a Roth IRA might be a preferable choice is when an individual is close to retirement and may not have enough time before the withdrawal phase to properly fund the life insurance option. Again, the situation is individualized, and a knowledgeable and properly licensed life insurance agent should easily be able to walk you through the best option for your specific situation.

#3 – Tax-Deferred Money

I don't need to belabor this point since we have already spent so much time in this book discussing the tax-deferred option. Too often people pour money into this category and have skipped over category #2 – *Tax-Free Money* – completely. In my opinion, that is a mistake. Remember, this is *The Smart Money Investment Order*™. Be smart!

#4 – Taxable Money

Just about everything else is taxable money which means it receives no tax breaks either now or in the future.

There you have it – *The Smart Money Investment Order*™.

Now let's explore the "second rule of money" before we jump into the technical aspects of how life insurance can provide its stellar strategy for long-term wealth accumulation. The "second rule of money" is this – *Less Tax is Better.* Yes, that does sound very elementary. And it is. But if it is so obvious, why are most people dumping money into accounts where they will pay more tax? Maybe they subscribe to a secret rule of money called *More Tax is Better.*

In order to illustrate this rule, I am going to use a series of graphs. These graphs will show, pictorially, what I have been describing verbally. For starters, please reference figure 18.3.

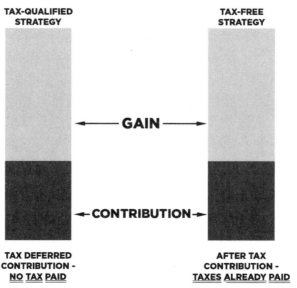

Figure 18.3

The first bar, on the left, represents a *tax-qualified* strategy such as a 401(k), 403(b), or IRA. The shaded part, at the bottom of the graph, represents the *contribution* that has been put into this account by the participant. As you can see, the majority of money in the account at maturity is *not* the money deposited but rather the growth on that money – the gain. As the graph shows, there has been *no tax paid on the shaded portion* – the contribution. But upon withdrawal **the entire account, both contribution and gain, gets fully taxed. Every cent.**

The second bar represents a *tax-free strategy* such as a Roth IRA or certain types of life insurance (if done properly). Unlike the shaded portion on the first graph, this shaded portion (contribution amount) is paid in *after-tax dollars*. In other words tax *has* already been paid on this money. The money is received by you in the form of your paycheck (taxes already taken out), and *then* it is placed into this accumulation vehicle. Just like the tax-qualified plan, most of the money in this strategy is generally gain, not contribution.

However, if this strategy is structured and utilized properly (based on current tax laws as of this writing), *an individual can access his money, both contribution and gain, without paying a single penny in tax.*

So the simple question you need to ask yourself is, "Would you rather pay tax on this?"

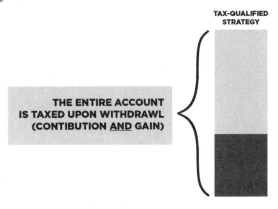

Figure 18.4

"Or this?

Figure 18.5

** I only address the Roth IRA in this book and not the Roth 401(k) for two reasons. One, in my experience the Roth 401(k) is offered to such a limited number of individuals that it really is not pertinent for most people reading this book, and I don't want to unnecessarily complicate the discussion. Secondly, although the growth inside of the Roth 401(k) may be tax-free, the government still has enough strings attached to it regarding access to the money that it does not give an individual all the freedom of choice that life insurance can offer, at least not at the present time. However, if you do have the Roth 401(k) option available to you, I encourage you to explore that as a viable and positive option.

Chapter 19

The Retirement Solution – Why Life Insurance?

The time has finally arrived for us to dive in and explore this new retirement strategy. All the chapters leading up to this point have had a significant purpose in laying a solid foundation upon which we can build.

You have trodden carefully through some common *Financial Landmines*™. You have explored the potential tax nightmare of tax-qualified retirement plans. And you clearly understand why a tax-free pot of money is better than a taxable pot of money. I'd say you're all set. Buckle your seat belt, and let's go! But as we do, please know that this is the most technical chapter in the book. You might need to slow down your reading pace or read this chapter twice to fully grasp the concept of how life insurance can provide you with a lifetime of tax-free income. However you do it, enjoy – because your financial future will never be the same.

There are many different kinds of permanent life insurance products available in the marketplace, but the type of product I believe best allows us to utilize all the benefits of this book is called Universal Life insurance. You've probably heard of it. You may even own it. This is a type of permanent insurance that has been sold by most major life insurance companies since the early 1980s, when it first entered the marketplace.

Here's how Universal Life insurance works. Just like any life insurance product, you pay a certain premium and receive a certain amount of death benefit. Traditionally, most agents and companies calculate the *minimum* premium needed to fund a certain amount of death benefit. This is the manner in which most policies have been sold to the public – the *most* life insurance for the *least* amount of money. This is also the reason why so many life insurance policies were in trouble in recent years. When a policy is funded at the *minimum premium* level, there is often not enough money being put into it to keep it alive until maturity, which is usually age 100 or later. Also, in the 1980s, when agents were illustrating interest-rate-based policies as high as 12%, 13%, or even 14%, the premiums collected were based on *projected* interest rates. As the following two decades played themselves out, however, interest rates didn't follow those highly projected targets. The interest rate pendulum swung completely in the other direction, leaving many of these minimally-funded policies gasping for air to stay alive. (As a side note: if the agents who originally sold these policies had conducted regular insurance reviews with their clients, these policies could have easily been spared an unnecessary death.)

The backlash of these poor sales strategies, along with this interest rate anomaly, has caused the public to dismiss what I believe is one of the most powerful accumulation strategies ever created.

In this situation the proverbial saying came to pass, and most Americans (as well as most financial planners) "threw the baby out with the bath water."

Let me illustrate a couple of different Universal Life funding options, beginning with what the vast majority of all life insurance clients choose to pay – the *minimum premium*. If a 40 year old male wanted to purchase $500,000 in life insurance death benefit and pay the *minimum premium* allowed by a company, he might expect to pay around $500 per month – give or take. If this 40-year-old male continued to make that $500 per month payment, he could potentially accumulate a cash value in the policy in the neighborhood of $300,000 at age 67.

If we look down the road a little further to age 85, the cash value could have potentially grown to $700,000 or more. And although this is a substantial sum, it is not the best way to utilize the policy... nor is it very exciting. Who likes buying life insurance? Who enjoys facing the prospect of their own death?

Let's face it. No one enjoys buying life insurance. Many people do it – very often willingly. But do they really enjoy it? No. Why should they? Who likes spending their own money today for someone else to receive a payoff after they are six feet under? That doesn't sound too exciting. I believe most people, even the responsible ones who willingly purchase this valuable protection for their families, see life insurance as, simply, a necessary evil. In fact I've had clients use that exact term more times than I can count.

Why do people feel this way about life insurance? The answer is simple. All the focus has been on the benefits provided to the family upon death. However wonderful those death benefits may be, the benefits that Universal Life insurance can provide *during* a person's lifetime are exponentially more exciting. Like I've mentioned many times in this book, most financial planners and insurance agents are not fully aware of the power of the available *living* benefits.

So let's turn the table 180 degrees and make this fun – a lot more fun. I want you to start by letting go of any previous knowledge you have of life insurance, whether fact or fiction. Clear your mind of those preconceived ideas so you can take a fresh look at a new concept. How would you feel if instead of $500 per month for $500,000 of life insurance you were told it was going to be $1,800 per month? You might cough and sputter. You might say that is way too expensive. You might even laugh, stand up, and walk out the door. (But probably not since you are likely a polite person.) But if you had any of those reactions, it would tell me you are still looking through an old, outdated lens, and that lens would be telling you that $1,800 a month is simply too much to pay for only $500,000 in death benefit. What I would tell you is, "It's time to put on a new lens."

When you put $1,800 into any other savings account, do you say to yourself, "You know, that is just way too much to pay for that savings account?" Of course not. Why? Because when you are *saving* money, it is not a purchase. You are simply putting money away, hopefully, to grow and provide you with a greater benefit in the future. As a matter of fact, a large monthly outlay for savings purposes is exciting, not depressing. The more you save, the more you hope to have in the future. And the longer you have to let it grow, and the more you can put into your account, the more powerfully Mr. Interest can labor for you.

So if a forty-year old male put $1,800 a month into a $500,000 life insurance policy, let's see what it could do for him. Depending on variations in policies, his cash value at age 67 could be as high as $1,500,000, with a death benefit of $2,000,000. Not bad. And if he kept contributing that same amount to his policy each year, he could potentially have a cash value of $5,000,000 and a death benefit of $5,500,000 at age 85 (his original $500,000 death benefit *plus* $5,000,000 cash value). Wow! That's some pot of money. But you might be saying to yourself, "Hold on a minute. If that money is still in the policy, how can it help him while he's living?"

Although the money is still in the policy, it is his money to do with as he pleases, similar to any other savings account he might possess. However, the most critical single factor in utilizing the power of life insurance comes with distribution. Accumulation is easy. Anyone can stuff these things full of money yet not fully realize the powerful tax advantages provided in them by Uncle Sam to *all* Americans, regardless of income, regardless of age, regardless of any other type of potentially discriminating factors. Would you like to have a completely tax-free retirement? Then read the next pages closely because they hold the secret.

Okay, so this individual has funded his life insurance to the maximum amount, as allowed by the tax laws, and he now has this big pot of money just waiting to be utilized. How does he get at it?

One option is that he can simply withdraw it. He can call up the company and sign a form letting them know he would like to cancel the policy, and they will send him the proceeds of his cash surrender value. So if we continue to use the example above, that means that at age 67 the life insurance company would cancel the policy and send him a check for $1,500,000. But he must hold his excitement. They also would send record of that large withdrawal to our friends at the IRS. And guess what? The IRS wants its share of the pie. In this case he put in $583,200 and drew out $1,500,000, leaving him a net profit of $916,800. That net profit would be taxed just like a distribution from an IRA. That doesn't sound like a good option, does it? Indeed it's not. At a 39.6% federal tax rate, the slice of pie the IRS would take would be $363,053. So withdrawing money in that fashion is no better than if he had saved money in a tax-qualified plan. As a matter of fact, it would be worse because life insurance did not provide him with the tax deferral on his original contributions. Okay, so it's clear he doesn't want to go that route. What other option does he have? A beautiful one!

Life insurance companies have set up a provision within their policy features that allows the client to take a loan against their cash value. Not *from* their cash value but *against* their cash value. Your initial reaction might be, "Ouch, that doesn't sound good during my retirement years. I don't want to be taking loans." But what if I told you that this loan charged you little to no interest and *never* needed to be paid back during your lifetime? Does that change the picture? You bet it does. Let's explore exactly how this loan works.

Again, using this same example, $583,200 of this individual's total pot of money consists of his original premium payments into the contract. The tax law regarding life insurance says that as long as a person has stayed under the contribution maximum (called the Modified Endowment Contract limit), then the first money withdrawn from their Universal Life insurance policy can come out tax-free, as a *withdrawal* (not a loan), *up to their total contribution amount*.

So in this case the client could withdraw $583,200 without paying any tax. Why? Because these dollars have already been taxed prior to being placed into the contract; they are simply a return of that premium. But that still leaves him with $916,800 to contend with. It's at this point that the *loan provision* gets employed.

Let's assume that at age 67 the total cash value in the policy of $1,500,000 could provide an annual income to this individual of $80,000, every year of his life until age 100. We know that he contributed $583,200 in premium payments to the policy, so that means that he could take *withdrawals* of $80,000 a year for seven years tax-free since that would simply represent a return of the life insurance premium he paid over the last twenty-seven years.

Wait! Did you catch the magnitude of what I just said? This individual *contributed* $583,200 into his policy over a 27-year period, yet with an $80,000 a year withdrawal, he would receive back income equaling his total premium in just *seven* short years. Think about that! He put money into this policy for 27 years, yet he would be able to receive it all back in income in just seven years. And you know what? In most cases there would still be virtually the same amount of cash value left in the policy at the end of those seven years as there was on the day he started taking the money out at age 67.

It is at this point that the loan provision begins. In this example, in the eighth year of withdrawals, the individual would still receive $80,000 a year tax-free from the life insurance company, but it would not come out in the form of a withdrawal from the policy; it would be given in the form of a loan from the insurance company itself.

Are loans taxed by the government? No. When you borrowed money to buy your car, was the loan taxed? No. The car was taxed but not the loan. When you borrowed money to buy your house, was the loan taxed? No. The same is true when a loan is taken from a life insurance company. The individual in this example would receive their $80,000 loan tax-free. Again ... zero tax!

But then what happens? The amount that is borrowed does get charged an interest rate, just like any other loan. For illustration sake lets assume that rate is 4%. So he is now getting charged 4% per year on his loan of $80,000. But that is only half of the story.

The life insurance company then removes that same exact amount of money out of his cash value and puts it into a separate account that earns 3 ½ to 4%. What's the net result? He is paying a net loan interest rate of somewhere between ½% and 0%. So what does this allow him to do? Through this provision he is able to continue to access his remaining cash value during his lifetime 100% tax-free, with little or no cost to him. It really doesn't get any better than that! Not only that, but since it is distributed as a loan, the withdrawal doesn't even show up on his annual tax return. As far as the IRS is concerned, it's invisible money that he gets to use throughout his entire lifetime, completely tax-free. Like I said, it's a beautiful thing.

The last component you need to understand is how the life insurance death benefit is taxed because it is the death benefit that makes this whole strategy work. Without an income-tax-free death benefit, neither this strategy nor this book would be in existence.

At death all the proceeds of a life insurance contract are paid to the beneficiary completely income tax free. Let's say, for this example, that the individual in our illustration lives to the age of 87. He would have withdrawn $80,000 tax-free every year from age 67. During those 20 years of withdrawals, he would have taken out $1,600,000 total in tax-free income. Even if his net interest rate was ½% on that $1,600,000 in tax-free income during those 20 years, at his death he could have his total loan paid off and, potentially, *still have an additional $1 million* (depending on the type of policy and options chosen) that would be paid to his named beneficiary – income tax free!

What does this mean? First of all, it means that he was able to live all of his retirement years without Uncle Sam seeing one red cent of his hard-earned money. Secondly, it means that at his death the loan would be paid off from a *portion* of the death benefit. And thirdly, after the loan was paid off, there would still be a significant amount of the death benefit left to be distributed to his beneficiaries (wife, children, grandchildren, charity, whomever). In this example it could easily be in the neighborhood of an additional $1,000,000 in income-tax-free proceeds that his beneficiaries would still receive *after* his tax-free loan was paid off.

In my world it just doesn't get any better than that! Tax-free dollars while you're living and tax-free dollars distributed to whomever you choose upon your death.

Right now, you're likely dying to ask two questions. "Okay, what's the catch?" And, "If this is so good, why isn't everyone doing this?"

To the first question I can only tell you there really is no catch. There is a caution, though, that I will cover shortly, but there is no catch. As long as you understand that you are buying life insurance – this is not like other savings plans – then there really isn't any catch. Most people need the life insurance anyway, so purchasing it in this format is a great way to get the life insurance they need and tax benefits they didn't know existed.

To the second question, "If this is so good, why isn't everyone doing this?" I can say the primary reason is that most people simply haven't heard about it. It is for this reason that I have written this book. It has been far too long that this great benefit has been hidden from mainstream America.

The second reason is that this strategy is not for everybody. Although it is *open* to everybody who can qualify for life insurance, it is best suited for a couple of target groups: those currently contributing to a tax-qualified plan such as a 401(k), SEP, SIMPLE, IRA, etc.; those who earn a relatively large income; and those who want to save more than the $5,500 a year that a Roth IRA currently allows.

In the next section I am going to explore four specific individual applications and why using life insurance for retirement savings is well suited for each one.

But before I jump to these applications, I previously mentioned that there is a caution in this plan that needs to be well heeded. The caution is this. Since it is the tax-free death benefit that makes this strategy work, it is **_imperative_** that the policy stays in force until the insured's death. That may sound pretty basic, but it is too important to gloss over. The reason the policy *must* stay in force is that *if the policy lapses or cancels, all that money the person has taken out as a tax-free loan suddenly becomes taxable,* and that is one tax bill you *never* want to see!

So how do you make sure the policy stays in force? Simple. First, don't take out too much money. When your agent runs income illustrations, make sure he or she runs them to at least age 100. Don't let someone try to show you better income projections by running them to only age 90 or 95. And if you think you are going to live past age 100, then take out less than the illustration shows.

Second, review your policy annually with the person who sold it to you. If your policy is returning less than the illustration predicted, then take out less money for a couple of years until it gets back on track with the illustration.

As a side note, make sure you buy this policy through a reputable agent who *fully* understands how this strategy works. Don't buy this type of policy over the internet or from an 800 number. You need the personal assistance of a qualified individual who will be able to walk you through the best distribution strategy possible.

Really, there is nothing to be scared of. You just need to show caution and discernment as you set up a successful distribution plan for your future.

* The numbers used in this chapter's example (cost, cash value, and death benefit) are fictitious and represent no particular type of policy or any particular company. These numbers are purely intended to introduce a concept and are not to be used for illustration purposes. Any similarities between these numbers and any actual policy are purely coincidental. Actual policy results can and will vary either positively or negatively based on the company, the type of policy, and the features chosen.

PART V: INDIVIDUAL APPLICATIONS

Chapter 20

Tax-Free Retirement™ for Physicians

In the next four chapters I want to explore specific applications for various groups of individuals who I believe would benefit most from this strategy.

I want to start this section with physicians, for a couple of reasons. My first reason is personal. I am the son of a doctor. My father retired seven years prior to the publication of my first edition of *Tax-Free Retirement*™ in 2007, after practicing medicine in the Northwest for over thirty-five years. He was a great doctor, loved by patients, hospital staff, and peers. And like all doctors he gave his life to his profession. I am a benefactor, in many ways, of growing up the son of a physician. I witnessed first-hand the significance of a great work ethic. I realized the importance of knowing your profession well. And most of all, I had the good fortune of growing up around a lot of truly wonderful people. Almost all of our closest friends were families within the medical community. I got to know doctors well. And though I chose not to follow in my father's footsteps, I desire to give something significant back to this community of individuals to whom I owe so much of who I am. Also, as I walked with my dad through his early years of retirement, the financial picture I witnessed, both for him and for others in this community, has been one of my chief reasons for wanting to offer this book to the public.

If my first reason is personal, my second reason is practical. Doctors have many unique attributes. And in my opinion, their unique attributes are what make this group one of the most significant to benefit from the strategies in this book. In this chapter I want to explore four key realities that make physicians such a fitting group to maximize the full benefit of this strategy. These four reasons are:

Reason #1

Most doctors make more than $196,000 per year, which is the phase-out limit for being able to contribute to a Roth IRA. Therefore, they have no truly viable tax-free retirement option available to them other than life insurance.

Reason #2

Doctors are specialists. They have given their lives to be the best at what they do – and they are. However, this level of specialty often leaves little time for less urgent activities such as retirement planning.

Reason #3

Doctors are often taken advantage of by snake-oil salesmen in the financial realm hocking half-baked, poorly-formed investment strategies promising wonderful returns.

Reason #4

Doctors generally need a lot of life insurance for three reasons. One, they need to protect a large income for their families. Two, they usually carry high debt. Often this is due to starting out in debt from large medical school bills and low wages during their residency and internship years. Three, doctors as a group have one of the lowest life expectancies of any profession.

That's the overview. I'd now like to look at each one of these reasons in more detail.

Reason #1 — *Most doctors make more than $196,000 per year, which is the phase-out limit for being able to contribute to a Roth IRA. Therefore, they have no truly viable tax-free retirement option available to them other than life insurance.*

Most doctors make a large income. And in my opinion, they deserve every dollar. Very few professionals invest so much for so long to provide such a wonderful service to the world. And unlike you and me in other lines of work, doctors can't have a bad day. A bad day can be deadly. That's a lot of pressure. Pressure most of the world chooses not to accept. Pressure that deserves to be well compensated.

And how does our tax system reward these individuals who take on the pressure to keep us all healthy? They penalize them by not allowing them to be able to contribute to one of the only tax-free investments offered to the public – the Roth IRA. And the reason? They make too much money.

However, even if a physician could contribute to a Roth IRA, it would fall far short of providing the necessary income to fund a lifestyle in retirement anywhere close to what they were used to during their working years.

So what options are available to doctors? They, like other high-income earners, can contribute to many of the standard tax-qualified retirement plans. Many medical partnerships and corporations set up their own pension and profit-sharing plans, but these too follow the tax rules of the other tax-qualified plans referenced earlier in this book. Also, each one of these plans has contribution caps that can be far lower than a doctor needs to fund a proper retirement, especially if you consider the amount the IRS is going to take upon withdrawal.

The other issue I have seen with doctors is that most of them have few business deductions. They often retain all the negative aspects of being a business owner, such as long hours, large responsibilities, and managing the financial books of a busy medical practice, yet they get few, if any, of the positive financial aspects that most business owners enjoy. I believe this lack of business deductions is a large reason why doctors pour their money into tax-qualified plans. They are easy justifications. Other than the regular personal deductions (which can also be phased out due to income level), a tax-qualified plan may be one of the only deductions a doctor can take on their tax return. With the huge tax bill that most physicians face each year, this is too large a carrot to pass up. But again, most have never stopped long enough to evaluate what the decision to fund a tax-qualified plan really means in their later years, once they stop working. It's certainly not something their plan administrator is going to readily share with them – they are often paid for assets under management. It's not something the government's going to tell them – it is greedily looking forward to the future taxes. And it's not something the doctor themself has much time to consider – he or she is too busy saving people's lives.

Let's pause for a minute and ask ourselves why the government would penalize high-income earners like physicians. It's simple. The government wants doctors to pump billions of dollars into tax-qualified plans because billions of dollars saved means hundreds of billions (or more) accumulated in the future that the government can get its hands on. And with a potential future tax rate of 50% or more for every dollar withdrawn from those accounts, the government is pretty excited about those tax-qualified plans. As I've asked before, whose retirement are doctors funding – the government's or their own? You have to stop and wonder.

Besides tax-qualified retirement plans, doctors do have other investment alternatives available to them, but most are either too time consuming, such as real estate, or do not provide tax advantages and can, therefore, create additional future tax liabilities.

So from the standpoint of viable investment alternatives available to the physician, we are left with only one real option. Luckily, it is one superior option – life insurance! For all the reasons we discussed in *Part IV, The Retirement Solution*, life insurance can be one of the most beneficial avenues for a physician's long-term retirement planning.

It can offer an unlimited contribution potential, all based on the size of the policy. It grows without annual taxation. It takes no time to manage. It provides a huge sum of money to the physician's family in the case of an untimely death. And best of all, if structured properly, the policy can allow access to future money tax-free.

I only wish someone had written this book twenty-five years ago for my father and all the other hard-working doctors that have long since retired. He would have been well served. However, my dad did what most other physicians have done – he socked as much money into his tax-qualified plan as the law would allow. And although my dad's pot of money grew to a rather large sum, he continues to be shocked at the disastrous one-two punch of heavy taxation and no tax deductions during his retirement years. He would have given anything to be able to withdraw his retirement income tax-free.

Reason #2 — *Doctors are specialists. They have given their lives to be the best at what they do – and they are. However, this level of specialty often leaves little time for less urgent activities such as retirement planning.*

With the schedules that doctors keep, they just don't have the time to research each financial opportunity to evaluate the risk-to-reward ratio. Physicians would be best served to stick with a proven strategy, especially one that can eliminate all future tax burdens.

Reason #3 — *Doctors are often taken advantage of by snake-oil salesmen in the financial realm hocking half-baked, poorly-formed investment strategies promising wonderful returns.*

It's funny how certain memories linger crystal clear from your childhood. For me some of those memories are the few failed investment endeavors of my father. Although he never included me in his financial decision making, I watched intently from afar. Limited partnerships gone bad. High-yield junk bonds defaulted. Condos that were held during a recession and then sold too soon.

Each one of these apparently legitimate investment opportunities were brought to him by a close friend or relative. Each one promised spectacular returns. Each one failed miserably.

Doctors often get targeted for these types of investments for a variety of reasons. Physicians tend to have a high trust factor. Because they are experts in their respective fields, they tend to trust other "experts" as well. However, as you know, not everyone who claims to be an expert in their field actually is one.

Additionally, they generally have enough discretionary money to put some at risk, and those seeking to put together these types of deals frequently take advantage of that knowledge.

Reason #4 – *Doctors generally need a lot of life insurance for three reasons. One, they need to protect a large income for their families. Two, they usually carry high debt. Often this is due to starting out in debt from large medical school bills and low wages during their residency and internship years. Three, doctors as a group have one of the lowest life expectancies of any profession.*

Doctors, of all people, should know how important it is to be well protected. They often see the devastating reminder of what happens to a family when it loses its primary breadwinner. And although doctors, by and large, do a better job than the general public in the arena of protecting themselves financially, I still find them vastly *underinsured* when it comes to life insurance.

As a general rule, an individual needs between seven and ten times their annual income in life insurance to properly protect their family left behind. Obviously, the larger the family and the more extravagant the lifestyle, the greater that figure becomes. I have seen one statistic that suggested the primary breadwinner carry as much as fourteen times their annual income in life insurance to be properly protected. Whatever the correct ratio is, I have found one thing to be true – most doctors need more life insurance than they currently have. In the past, this need could hang on them like a financial anchor. But now, if doctors understand this new way to utilize life insurance, they will realize that the more life insurance they purchase, the more money they are also able to accumulate for retirement.

Chapter 21

Tax-Free Retirement™ for Business Owners

As I mentioned in the last chapter, part of my motivation for writing this book was to serve the medical community that my father was a part of for so many wonderful years. Another primary reason for this book was to address the dire needs of small-business owners who, in my opinion, are hugely underserved in the financial landscape. I know this because I am part of this group of individuals. We are ignored. Forgotten. Left to fend for ourselves. Why is this the case? Easy answer. We are not worth the trouble for most benefit specialists. I have some friends who own an employee benefits company, and they have told me, on more than one occasion, it's not worth their time or energy to work with businesses that have less than one hundred employees. Groups of one hundred or larger are not much more work than a small group of four, yet the profits to *their* business are vastly different, as you might imagine. So, from a business standpoint, their efforts make perfect sense – for *their* bottom line.

However, this lack of pursuit of the small-business owner by financial experts has left a vacuum in the marketplace. And how does this vacuum manifest itself? Does it surprise you that most small-business owners have set up no type of retirement plan for themselves? Nothing. They know they should. They know time is passing quickly, but they do what we all do – procrastinate. Unfortunately, the future has a way of sneaking up on us like a rabid wolf. And many business owners find themselves ready to retire without the financial means to do so.

I believe there are some unique reasons why it can be harder for the small-business owner to get started putting money away for retirement than for other professionals.

First of all, since money is lean in the early years, the business owner doesn't begin a habit of saving right from the start.

Second, a small-business owner is often pursued by no one. They are left to fend for themself in this financial jungle. Once they are successful they are pursued, but by that time many are close to retirement with no money saved, or they are solely dependent upon their business' income or its subsequent sale to provide for their retirement income.

Third, the business is hungry. There is always something that is calling for more cash. More employees. More marketing. More inventory. More research and development. What often happens is that the owner is the last one on the list to get paid. And when they finally do start getting paid, there is often a list of financial priorities screaming so loudly that retirement's soft whisper never gets heard.

Fourth, similarly to the doctor, most of the time a business owner starts their business by acquiring substantial debt. This debt eats into their profit margins for years before there is enough left over to begin saving.

Fifth, most of the time a business owner is so engrossed in starting and running their company that they haven't taken the time to research where they would save money, even if they could.

Sixth, and maybe most significantly, a business owner who can and would save money for retirement often doesn't want to use tax-qualified plans because funding a plan for themself means they usually need to fund it for their employees as well. This does not always sit well with a small-business owner, especially in a cash-starved business.

So how does using life insurance overcome all of these obstacles? Let's find out.

One common thread that was woven throughout many of the above six reasons is the issue of debt. Small-business owners generally take on substantial debt. And although my next statement is a generalization I cannot substantiate, I do believe it to be true. The generalization is this: most small-business owners have a family. Does this cause any bells to go off in your head? It certainly does in mine, but I am in the business of risk management. High debt plus family dependents add up to the need for one thing – life insurance. Obviously, the need for life insurance for debt protection has nothing to do with retirement income, but rather, it has everything to do with taking care of the loved ones left behind.

And while doctors, as a whole, might be *moderately* underinsured, small-business owners, in my opinion, are often *grossly* underinsured and, in many cases, completely *uninsured*. Why? For the same reasons given above – tight cash flow in their businesses and little attention given to them by the financial community.

So why might life insurance be the ideal retirement solution for the business owner? Let's highlight the reasons, before we look in more detail.

Reason #1

A business owner needs life insurance to cover their business debt and to provide for their family if he or she were to die. Therefore, owning a life insurance policy is not an *extra* but, rather, something that should be a standard part of every business owner's portfolio.

Reason #2

The business itself usually provides plenty of deductions during the accumulation phase of a business owner's life, so the desire for additional tax deductions, such as a tax-qualified plan, is often minimized. Conversely, a retired business owner often finds themself with few or no tax write-offs since the business has been sold, creating the desperate need for tax-advantaged income in retirement.

Reason #3

Since, according to the IRS, life insurance is *not* considered a tax-qualified plan, there is *no requirement* for the business owner to fund a similar plan for their employees.

Reason #4

There is no government-enforced limit as to how much can be saved within a life insurance contract; it is only limited by what the contract itself specifies. Since business income can change dramatically over the years, this flexibility can be a big advantage.

Reason #5

It's simple and easy. There are no separate record keeping or tax forms required. As a matter of fact, Uncle Sam doesn't generally know when an individual policy even exists. There is *no* reporting requirement.

Reason #6

It provides instant liquidity (for pennies on the dollar) to the owner's heirs or estate if the owner decides to keep the business until their death.

Pretty significant list, isn't it? This is all in addition to my personal belief that life insurance provides the most tax-advantaged, low-maintenance, fully-liquid saving strategy on the planet.

So let's look at each of these six reasons in more detail.

Reason #1 — *A business owner needs life insurance to cover their business debt and to provide for their family if he or she were to die. Therefore, owning a life insurance policy is not an extra but rather something that should be a standard part of every business owner's portfolio.*

The first reason is pretty self-explanatory, and we have touched on it in the paragraphs above. A business owner needs life insurance. Why? To cover their debt and to allow their family to continue to live an adequate lifestyle if he or she were to die prematurely.

Reason #2 — *The business itself usually provides plenty of deductions during the accumulation phase of a business owner's life, so the desire for additional tax deductions, such as a tax-qualified plan, is often minimized. Conversely, a retired business owner often finds themself with few or no tax write-offs since the business has been sold, creating the desperate need for tax-advantaged income in retirement.*

Let's explore the issue of tax write-offs for the small-business owner. If you're a small-business owner, you are faced with a barrage of expenses at every turn. And in your world expenses equate to tax write-offs. Income *reduction* is not difficult; income *creation* is. As a matter of fact, there are some businesses whose entire profits are gobbled up by expenses. If you are a business owner, you know, all too well, that you are not in the same boat as the doctor who has a high income and no tax write-offs. Not only are you not in the same boat, you may not even be sailing in the same ocean. Your struggle is just the opposite – plenty of tax write-offs and not enough income.

Granted, this is a vast generalization, for I know many wealthy business owners whose income far outpaces that of any physician on the planet. And in order to defer current taxation, many of these successful business owners employ high-powered accountants and attorneys to legitimately design ways within their businesses to minimize their current personal incomes. But again, this is often just a deferral technique, not an avoidance technique. And what happens when you defer taxes? You tend to compound them, thereby making them worse.

So both successful business owners and modest business owners share this common thread – reducing current income taxation today is not the highest financial priority, for that can be done in many other ways. What *is* a top priority is having a flexible savings plan that allows them to dump future profits into that can be designed to avoid taxation when it counts the most – once the business is sold and the expenses have evaporated.

So what does this mean in relation to life insurance? A perfect fit! As we have discussed, life insurance does not provide tax deductibility for contributions today, but if designed properly, it can provide tax-free income when the business owner needs it the most.

Reason #3 — *Since, according to the IRS, life insurance is not considered a tax-qualified plan, there is no requirement for the business owner to fund a similar plan for their employees.*

The beauty of life insurance is this – it is *not* a tax-qualified retirement plan. Therefore, it does not fall under the regulation of tax-qualified plans; this leaves the business owner, himself, as the sole determinant of whose retirement gets funded. If an employer wants to put away money for his employees, he can. However, if he is in a position in which he is not able to do so, or doesn't want to, he doesn't have to. The key is this – the business owner has the freedom to choose. There are no funding regulations imposed upon them by the powers-that-be at the federal level. It is completely *their* decision!

If you are a business owner, let me ask you, "Isn't the power to make your own decisions one of the reasons you went into business for yourself in the first place?"

I thought so.

Reason #4 — *There is no government-enforced limit as to how much can be saved within a life insurance contract; it is only limited by what the contract itself specifies. Since business income can change dramatically over the years, this flexibility can be a big advantage.*

When a business owner sells their business, what do they do with the proceeds? Great question, isn't it? Most business owners never stop to ask this question because they are running so fast trying to *build* a business they might actually be able to sell one day. But now that I've asked it, let's spend a minute thinking about it. Where can a business owner invest the proceeds, from the sale of their business, that offers any tax-favored status?

Can the money be put into a tax-qualified retirement plan? No. What about a pension or profit-sharing plan? Double no. What about a Roth IRA? Once again, no. Why? Because these plans have contribution limits. And if a contribution is not deposited in the current year in which it is earned, it is lost forever. Therefore, none of the above plans are adequately suited to receive the large sum of money that could arise from the eventual sale of a business.

Once again, this is not the case with life insurance. Life insurance not only provides a completely flexible plan in which a business owner can vary premium amounts from year to year, but it allows the business owner to *make up for previously missed contributions,* if cash flow improves in the future. And most importantly, it can be structured to create a bucket big enough to hold some, most, or even all of the proceeds from the eventual sale of the business and allows the business owner to put those sale proceeds to work in a tax-favored manner.

Reason #5 — *It's simple and easy. There are no separate record keeping or tax forms required. As a matter of fact, Uncle Sam doesn't generally know when an individual policy even exists. There is no reporting requirement.*

The last thing a business owner needs is more record keeping. Running a business is a full-time job. Think of all the record keeping that comes into play – federal tax, state tax, business and occupation tax, employment security, labor and industry, keeping track of inventory, calculating payroll, compiling marketing budgets and sales forecasts, and a million other things to keep track of. The last thing a business owner wants or needs is more record keeping or form filing.

Let me make this simple. If utilized properly, life insurance has no record-keeping requirements. That's right – none – other than what the policyowner, himself, desires.

Let's suffice to say that no other alternative offers anything close to the simplicity of life insurance record keeping requirements. Many other plans are as cumbersome as a bipartisan budget proposal.

Reason #6 — *It provides instant liquidity (for pennies on the dollar) to the owner's heirs or estate if the owner decides to keep the business until their death.*

If I told you I would trade you one dollar for every three cents you gave me, would you do it? How many of those trades would you make? What if I said you could make as many trades as you wanted? If you were smart, you would make as many as you could. You'd be giving up pennies and making dollars. Not a bad way to create wealth in very short order.

Welcome to the world of life insurance. In its most basic terms, it is simply trading pennies for dollars. As a business owner, that sounds pretty good to me.

So what if your plan, as a business owner, does not include retirement or selling your business? Instead, maybe your path is one that thousands before you have taken. You plan to draw income from the business until your death and then hand the business down to your children. That is a great plan and often works well. There is just one major obstacle in your way. Taxes.

At your death the value of your personal business interests will be included in your estate, and since it is included in your estate, it will be taxed – and taxed heavily. Most parents, who are kind enough to pass the family business down to their children, are not the type of individuals who want to burden them with huge tax bills that can't be paid.

So how can you avoid taxation? For all intents and purposes, you can't. Yes, there are convoluted ways to pass on a business entity to heirs prior to death that can help with the taxation picture, but they bring in other complicating factors. And quite frankly, most business owners do not take the time or money to explore those options. Most business owners die and the business value is added to their estate. So their new-owner child has to come up with a large amount of cash to pay the taxes so they can keep and take over the family business. Where is this cash going to come from? Most business owners have poured their life savings into the equity of the business and have not amassed large amounts of cash to cover this type of need, so the estate is often cash poor and business rich ... that is unless the business owner has purchased life insurance – preferably permanent life insurance.

The reason permanent life insurance is so much more appropriate than term life insurance in this particular circumstance is because many business owners will live longer than a term policy will stay in existence. If they outlive the coverage, it does them no good. Not only will they have wasted a lot of money in premium, but they will have nothing to show for it. Not a great combination on the wisdom scale.

So even if you live a long life and don't plan to use insurance as a retirement savings vehicle, the need for permanent life insurance, as a business owner, is still very significant. It's purchasing dollars for pennies, and every business owner likes the sound of that.

Chapter 22

Tax-Free Retirement™ for Tax-Qualified Plan
Contributors and High-Income Earners
(and Everyone Else)

Obviously, individual applications for different professions have many commonalities and overlaps. It would have been easy for me to identify six or seven target groups and give each one its own chapter. The risk in this would have been mindless repetition, chapter after chapter, of similarities. Doctors have some unique characteristics and business owners have some unique characteristics, but none of them are completely unique to either. More than likely, as you read the last two chapters, you identified with characteristics that resonated with your own life as well.

So the question I faced at this point in the book was, "How can I capture the remaining applications without stretching this section out to six or seven more repetitive chapters to fit each and every individual need?"

I decided that highlighting the primary characteristics for each, in an easy-to-review format, was the best solution.

It is my belief that the ideas and principles set forth in this book can benefit just about anyone. And for this reason my first draft titled this chapter *Tax-Free Retirement™ for Everyone Else*. As true as this title may be, I realized that the principles of this book particularly apply to three groups of individuals:

- Tax-Qualified Plan contributors
- High-income households making more than $196,000 per year ($133,000 if single)
- Individuals who want to save more than $5,500 per year in a tax-favored environment (everyone else)

If you've gotten to this point in the book, then these three groups should certainly be no surprise to you. Most of our attention has been given to one of these three groups. Also, if at this point you are not captivated by this new way of saving for your future, then this chapter will do little to move you further in that direction.

However, if you are anxious to explore more and see if this is an avenue that fits well with your dreams and desires, then this chapter may be just what you need, as a review, to bring some added clarity to the picture.

What I'd like you to do is personalize the next section. Get a pen or pencil, and get ready to mark up this book. I'd like you to put a check mark next to each of the statements that are true for you. If you find yourself having checked off more than two or three of these boxes, then very likely, this is a strategy that can serve you very well.

Do you have your pen ready? Okay, let's go…

- ☐ I am someone who wants to receive tax-free income during retirement.
- ☐ I am someone who has a need for life insurance.
- ☐ I am someone who wants to save more per year than what a Roth IRA allows.
- ☐ I am someone who is currently investing in a tax-qualified plan *above the company-matched contribution.*
- ☐ I am someone who is contributing to a deferred compensation plan.
- ☐ I am someone who makes more than $133,000 per year.
- ☐ I am someone who has a desire to multiply my assets for the benefit of my family or something I believe in.
- ☐ I am someone who has at least 12-15 working years left before I plan to retire.

Did you check any boxes? Was it two or more? If so, then the real question is: what do you do next? Here's my suggestion.

You will never know how well this really fits for you until you meet with a properly licensed and qualified life insurance producer who can evaluate your individual needs and then recommend what is best for you – *not* what is best for them. It's very likely that a licensed life insurance agent that you already know gave you this book because they believe you fit the profile of someone who could benefit greatly from this concept. If you like what you've read, then please take the time to visit with them. It may just change the rest of your financial life.

As you pick someone to work with, choose someone who is knowledgeable, whom you like, and whom you trust. Not only will they serve you in the best manner, but the entire discovery process will be a wonderful adventure.

I have had individuals sitting at my desk, eager to give me

a lot of money in order to buy a life insurance policy for wealth accumulation purposes, but have had to look them squarely in the eyes and advise them that, in their particular situation, it was *not* the best strategy. Could I have sold them the policy? More than likely. They were practically throwing the money at me because of something a friend or relative had told them. But the bottom line is – it wasn't the right fit *for them.*

I share this story with you simply to say, work with someone who will not be afraid to walk away from the sale, to tell you honestly that something else might fit you better. If you get the sense that you are a round peg they are trying to force through a square hole, then stop, step back, and find another agent or advisor who will put *your* wellbeing before their pocketbook.

And one note of caution on this. Don't be afraid to work with a highly successful agent. Those who do the best job for others usually end up being the most successful themselves. It's one of those idiosyncratic laws of business.

Now for the other side of the coin. Who may *not* be a good candidate for this type of strategy?

- Someone who has *no* need for life insurance as a death benefit **and** does not desire to save more than a Roth IRA will allow
- Someone whose health will not allow them to qualify for life insurance
- Someone whose age or health makes the cost of life insurance disproportional to the cash accumulation benefits
- Someone who plans to fund this strategy for less than 12-15 years

Which camp do you find yourself in?

Chapter 23

Tax-Free Retirement™ for Children and Grandchildren

Do you remember the illustration about the penny or the one about the sale of Manhattan? What do both of these illustrations have in common? The power of time.

In your retirement planning right now, you are dealing with three variables: amount contributed, rate of growth, and time. What if you could eliminate the third variable altogether? Well, I guess it can never be truly eliminated, but what if you could minimize it to the point of insignificance? Would you do it? Of course you would. Well, the good news is that you can – maybe not for yourself, but certainly for the generations that follow.

One of the other major downfalls of tax-qualified retirement plans is they are limited solely to workers. How many three-year-old workers have you seen in the marketplace? For that matter how many 18, 19, or 20 year olds do you know who are saving for retirement? Not many, I can assure you.

Do you remember the chart depicting the saving habits of Jill and Mark? Jill contributed $2,000 from age 19 to age 26 and then stopped, while Mark contributed the same annual amount from age 27 to age 65. Who won? Jill. Why? Time!

What would the same chart have looked like if Jill's parents or grandparents had started saving $2,000 per year for her when she was born? The numbers become mind-numbing. If her parents or grandparents would have saved $2,000 per year for eighteen years and then stopped contributions forever, at age 65 she would have an account balance of $8,847,811, using the same 10% interest rate from Mark and Jill's comparison. Stunning! And this nearly $9 million in assets would have grown from a total contribution of only $36,000, all contributed by her eighteenth birthday. That accumulation amount is ten times greater than Mark's, even though he contributed more than double that amount ($78,000) over the course of 39 years.

So why life insurance? Aren't there other things that parents and grandparents can invest in for their children and grandchildren?

Yes, but once again, the other alternatives face a blizzard of downfalls – regular taxation, massive record keeping, and complicated ownership regulations just to name a few.

In my opinion, there really aren't any great options... except for life insurance. As a matter of fact, I think life insurance may just be the *perfect* option.

- It has no age or income requirements for contributions; you can purchase it for your child or grandchild the week after they are born and let it accumulate during all of those additional decades of their life.

- It grows without annual taxation; there are no pesky tax bills to be paid.
- The money can be accessed tax-free if done properly.
- It is incredibly flexible; you decide the payment schedule.
- The actual insurance cost is very inexpensive because it is based on the age of a child.
- You decide when (if ever) to transfer ownership to the child; you can hold it during those tumultuous teens and twenties.
- And best of all, unless your child has some significant health issues when they are born, they should qualify for insurance. This may not be the case in their adult years if health issues arise.

This could be the greatest gift a parent or grandparent could bestow upon the next generation. Would you like to be remembered for giving your child or grandchild a gift they could never duplicate or repay? A gift that will produce a harvest long after you are gone? A gift that will likely foster similar generosity for generations to come? And a gift that could make a difference in the lives of thousands ... if your child or grandchild follows the principles set forth in Chapter 25?

If that sounds good, then happy gift giving!

PART VI: THE NEXT STEP

Chapter 24

Turbo Charging Tax-Free Retirement™ – IRA Rescue

My guess is that you didn't know your IRA needed rescuing. Let me assure you – it does! But the vast majority of people don't know what it needs to be rescued *from*. Any guesses? How about our old friend, Uncle Sam? There are many IRAs in people's portfolios that desperately need to be rescued from the tax hatchet.

For a moment, I want to divide money into three different categories: *now money*, *later money*, and *never money*.

Now money is money that you plan to spend today.

Later money is money that is going to be saved for some time in the future, whether that future is in a few months, a few years, or a few decades.

Never money is just that – money that is sitting in some account never to be spent. For those of you in the accumulation phase of life or whose retirement account is under-funded, this may be a hard concept to understand, but you would not believe how common it is. A large number of individuals have money sitting in an account they never plan to spend. They call it their "rainy day" account. Their emergency account. Their security fund. Who knows what they call it, but one thing's for sure – they *never* plan to spend it. They'd rather die than touch it. And where do you think a huge portion of this *never money* sits? You guessed it. In IRAs. There's only one problem. The IRS won't allow that money to sit there and never be touched.

Do you remember our discussion about what happens on April 1st of the year after you turn age 70 ½? The IRS *forces* you to begin taking systematic withdrawals from that IRA each year. It does seem a bit silly, doesn't it? Having someone tell you that you *have* to spend your money by a certain age – money you may not need or want or know what to do with.

But once again, there is another way, and that's the IRA Rescue.

What do you think the purpose is for most people's *never money*? Why would someone want to leave money in an account, without touching it, until their death? Although people will say it's for a rainy day or for emergencies or for a general sense of security, when you dig deeper you usually find it is there to pass on to their heirs. Many people want to leave something behind for their children or grandchildren. Unfortunately, not only is an IRA *not* a good way to pass money on to heirs, it is one of the *worst* possible ways to pass on money. Again, as we discussed before, at death an IRA gets taxed as income (at the appropriate tax bracket) before it gets passed on to the heirs. So if there is a substantial amount left in an IRA and the individual lives in a state with a state tax, then nearly 50% (by today's tax rates) could be chopped off the top before the heirs see a single penny. And you know my other bias; I believe these tax rates will be even higher in the future.

Do you think this is really how these individuals want their money distributed? Is that how *you* want your money distributed? Not a chance. So let's again put the amazing power of life insurance to work, along with the incredible benefit of its income tax-free payout at death.

Remember, the IRS is going to *force* you to begin taking money from your IRA on April 1st of the year after you turn age 70 ½. But with the strategy I'm about to show you, that no longer poses a problem. Actually, that mandatory distribution provides you with the power to multiply your IRA in ways you never dreamed of.

If you are an individual who has a *never money* account and that money is in an IRA, then *please read carefully.* How would you like to multiply the amount of money you pass on to your heirs and, at the same time, minimize the amount of tax your heirs will pay? Sounds pretty attractive, doesn't it? How can you do that? I'll show you.

You know those frustrating mandatory distributions? What do you think they could be used for? How about annual life insurance premiums? Think about it. The government is forcing you to take money out of an account you don't really want to liquidate, so let's turn the table on Uncle Sam and use those distributions to buy an even larger sum of money. Here's how.

Let's say you have $100,000 in an IRA that you never intend to spend. It's there for security only. It's just sitting, growing in value. But once you reach the mandatory distribution age, the IRS says you *must* take a certain amount of money out and not just once but *every year.*

What's usually the largest obstacle that stands in the way of life insurance? Finding the money to pay the annual premium. But what do these mandatory distributions give you? They give you a "built-in" annual premium from money you don't need, don't want, and don't know what to do with! As a matter of fact, the best way to structure this life insurance policy is to calculate the amount of life insurance based upon the amount of annual income that the Required Minimum Distribution provides.

And you don't need to stick to just the minimum distribution amount. In many cases the account may generate a substantial annual income from growth or interest. And this annual income could produce enough money to buy two or three times the value of your IRA in life insurance. And remember, that large death benefit will be paid to your beneficiaries in *income tax-free* dollars upon your death.

Now you may be thinking, "That sounds great, but I don't want to give up access to my money in case I *do* need it." Don't worry! If you utilize Universal Life insurance, then much of the money that gets paid into the life insurance policy, as annual premiums, is still accessible to be withdrawn if an emergency or unforeseen need arises. It's just about the perfect strategy.

So by rescuing your IRA, what have you done? You have used the negative aspect of the mandatory distribution to your advantage. You have multiplied the amount of money you will pass on after your death by a significant factor. You still retain liquidity of your money during your lifetime for the desired security you seek. And lastly, don't forget that you still have the original IRA. Who knows how much will be left in it? If you have only taken out the Required Minimum Distribution each year, it will be the same amount regardless of whether you bought the life insurance or not. In my world that is called having your cake and eating it too.

Once again, people are quick to ask, "What's the catch?" And again, I will unequivocally say, "There is no catch!" But there may be a reason that everyone you know isn't doing this, and that reason is, simply, because most people don't have a *never money* account. They need everything they have just to live from month to month. But if you are one of those few individuals that does indeed have a *never money* account, this is the most sure-fire and significant way to multiply the amount of money you can pass on to others while utilizing a built-in way to pay for the annual life insurance premium. This is an ideal option for a person who has money sitting in an account that they want to pass on to the next generation, to a charity, or to some other organization upon their death.

TAX-FREE RETIREMENT

Chapter 25

Leaving a Legacy

I believe every human being wants to know one thing. Will my life make a difference? It's the foundational question we ponder on those occasional sleepless nights. It's a question unique to the human race. Birds don't ask it. Fish don't ask it. Monkeys don't ask it. At the end of our life we want to know: did I leave my mark? Was my life significant? Did I make a difference in the lives I touched during my time on earth? It's simply the way we were created. We can ignore the question. We can side-step the question. We can deny the question. But we will never escape the question. It will follow us until our last breath. And that is a good thing because we were *created* to make a difference. We were created *on* purpose and *for* a purpose.

But the ironic thing is that life has a funny way of derailing us from our most significant pursuits. Our grandest dreams are replaced with mortgage payments. Our loftiest desires are traded in for the daily grind. And the purity of our youthful convictions are swapped for the messiness of real life.

Before we know it, we reach the twilight years of life. The kids are grown. The mortgage is paid. The career is in the rearview mirror. It is then that our heart dares to speak again. And what does it speak? The same question that has been branded on it since birth. *Did my life make a difference?*

If we examine our lives too harshly, we can easily beat ourselves up for all the lost opportunities. For the times we were greedy instead of generous. For the times we spoke harshly instead of graciously. For the times we were demanding instead of patient. For the myriad opportunities to make a difference when we did nothing. The wasted years. The forgotten dreams. The unspoken words.

We can actually come to a point in our lives in which we believe that our opportunity to make a difference is gone forever. If you are in this season of life or know someone in this season of life, take heart. It is *never* too late to make a difference! This chapter is all about making your life count. And you can. No matter how the past has played out, your future can make a significant difference in the lives of thousands. And that is not an exaggeration. You can leave a lasting impact on the world for generations to come.

I have been involved with charities and nonprofit organizations for over 30 years. And you know what? There is one common thread linking each of these organizations. Every one of them needs money. Their work is hampered by a lack of funding. It's astounding for me to think about how much more work could be accomplished through these organizations if the issue of money was completely taken off the table. Countless lives would be served. Millions would be fed, clothed, cared for, and ministered to. Money is the great obstacle for every charitable organization in the world. But it doesn't have to be. You see, these organizations' shortfalls are not money problems. They are heart problems.

In no way do I want this chapter to *guilt* people into giving. Not at all. It is my desire that as people, once again, embrace the real question of their hearts, they will be *inspired* to give. That they will look for ways to multiply their wealth for the generations to follow. And the exciting thing is that it can be done very simply. You can invest now in such a way as to make a lasting and significant difference in untold lives for decades to come.

It is my hope that, during my lifetime, I could inspire thousands of individuals to cheerfully give billions of dollars to charity and that those billions of dollars would feed the hungry, clothe the poor, help the illiterate to read, and minister to the hurting and lonely. And there is not one part of me that believes this is too lofty of a goal.

Do you want to make a difference? Do you want to make your life and wealth count? If so the good news is that you can.

Knowing this book has centered on the miracle of life insurance, it should be no surprise to you that, once again, we will employ it to empower this new vision for our lives to make a difference. What you have read so far in this book gets you ninety-nine percent there. We are left with just the last critical one percent. And this last one percent *is* critical, for it is not how we begin a race that matters but rather how we finish it that counts.

This reminds me of a story from the 1968 Olympics. A full hour after the winner of the Olympic marathon had crossed the finish line, Tanzania's John Stephen Akhwari limped across the finish line, injured from a fall early in the race. Asked why he didn't quit, he said, "My country didn't send me 7,000 miles to start the race. My country sent me here to finish the race."[xix]

Just like that runner I believe we all want to finish strong. We spend the first 26 miles of our lives acquiring and accumulating. But then it comes down to the last few yards. The last one percent. And what is that last one percent of our race in a financial sense? It is *distribution.*

So *what* are you going to leave behind, and to *whom* are you going to leave it?

Pause for a moment and ask yourself a question. And I don't mean in the rhetorical sense. Really. Pause and see which of these visions cause your heart to beat a little faster. When you die, would you rather leave your wealth to your kids, so they can buy a nicer car or a larger house, or would you like to designate your wealth in such a way as to become a champion for the less fortunate – build houses for the homeless, feed the hungry, bring hope to the hopeless – knowing that each life you touch will be replicated in other lives touched through the centuries? Doesn't the second scenario give you a renewed sense of significance?

If you utilize life insurance for building a *Tax-Free Retirement*™ or for performing an *IRA Rescue,* as this book describes, you will likely find there will be an abundance of money still in your policy long after it is needed for your own uses. So what do you do with all of this money? Who's going to receive that wealth? Who will you transfer it to?

Without thinking through possible options, many people just naturally pass all of it on to their children, grandchildren, or other living relatives. And please hear me; there is nothing wrong with passing money on to your children or relatives, especially if there are needs that exist in their lives. But for most of us our kids will have enough. They really don't need more. Our inheritance will become more troublesome than helpful. Trust me. I can't tell you the number of individuals and families I've seen torn apart by the distribution of a parent's wealth. Aren't our family relationships much more important than money? Of course. Not only that, but as we give out of a lofty vision for the hurting of this world, many of our children will follow suit. We can, therefore, not only leave a legacy of money; we can, more importantly, leave a legacy of the *spirit of giving.*

In reality some of our wealth will be passed on to our heirs, but it's not an all-or-nothing proposition. What if part of your money went to an organization you are currently passionate about? Think how fun that phone call would be. Let's say you are passionate about providing for the needs of the poor in this world. One organization doing great work is World Vision, based out of the Seattle area. Let's say this is one of the organizations you choose to leave money to. The conversation might go something like this:

"Hi. Could I please speak to the president of World Vision?"

"Sure, just a moment please."

"Hello." A new voice says.

"Hi there. You don't know me, and I wasn't sure whom to talk with in your organization, so I decided to start at the top. I love what your organization is doing for the needy and hurting around the world, and I want to assign you 50% of my life insurance policy so that, when I die, a portion of my estate will go directly to your organization."

Silence.

"Hello? Are you still there?" you ask.

"Yes, I'm sorry. I don't know what to say. That is incredibly generous. Thank you."

"My pleasure. Thanks for what your organization continues to do around the world. I'm proud to give to something that makes such a tremendous difference."

"Your words are very kind. Thank you. Before you go, though, could I ask a pragmatic question regarding your gift?"

"Sure. What's that?"

"Obviously, since it's life insurance proceeds, I know the gift won't be given until some time in the future, but how much might this amount to?"

"Well, I don't have an exact number because the total benefit amount will continue to change into the future, but it should be in the neighborhood of three to four million."

After a long, protracted silence. "You're kidding, right? Did I miss something? In all my life I've never had a call like this before."

"No. Truly, this isn't a joke. I want my life to make a difference, even after I am gone, and I believe your organization embodies my vision to do just that. Please use the money wisely and make a difference in as many lives as you can. Thank you."

How would that be for your swan song? I can only imagine how much fun that day will be.

How do you do this? It's simple. All you have to do is update your beneficiary form to designate what percentage you want to go to which person or organization. That's it! That's the last one percent of the race. The distribution of our money will be the point in which we cross our financial finish line. And nothing could be more simple than directing life insurance proceeds. There are no high-cost legal fees. There are no complicated tax ramifications. There are no lengthy forms to fill out. Just a simple change of beneficiary and it's done.

As a side note, this idea of charitable giving can be taken to even greater lengths using an assortment of different kinds of trusts, but the scope of this chapter is not set up to adequately deal with the complexities of that topic. This chapter is simply intended to enlarge your vision. To help you answer the question of your heart, "Did my life make a difference?"

My desire is that you *will* be able to answer that question with a resounding, "Yes! My life did make a difference!" Use the power of life insurance to multiply your wealth. Then use that wealth to bring comfort to countless lives that have been cast aside by our world.

Dream big! Make a difference! And leave a legacy!

Disclosure

The views, opinions, and hypothetical examples in this publication are not meant to provide specific financial, insurance, or investment advice. Please consult with a trained and licensed financial professional to discuss your unique risk tolerance, time horizons, financial objectives, and retirement goals.

Please note the illustrations in this book are purely conceptual in nature. They are intended to expand your financial knowledge, not to provide you with any type of personal or investment instruction. While the concepts can work beautifully if managed properly, even the best plan can be grossly mismanaged and turn out a complete disaster. It all depends on wise choices and proper execution.

Also, as obvious as this may sound, this book was written in the present, not the future. While the concepts in it worked the day it was written, there is no promise they will continue to be true in the future. While it is my hope these concepts will stand the test of time, tax laws are continually altered to meet the changing needs of our society and economy. So, once again, this book is simply intended to move you in the right direction; a direction that finds you seeking advice from a qualified professional, who can guide you along through the years in a well-managed and capable fashion.

Lastly, each method of utilizing your policy's cash value has advantages and disadvantages and is subject to different tax consequences. Surrenders of, withdrawals from, and loans against a policy will reduce the policy's cash surrender value and death benefit and may also affect any dividends paid on certain policies. As a general rule, surrenders and withdrawals are taxable to the extent they exceed the cost basis of the policy, while loans are not taxable when taken.

Loans taken against a life insurance policy can have adverse effects if not managed properly. Policy loans and automatic premium loans, including any accrued interest, must be repaid in cash or from policy values upon policy termination or the death of the insured. Repayment of loans from policy values (other than death proceeds) can potentially trigger a significant tax liability and there may be little or no cash value remaining in the policy to pay the tax. If loans equal or exceed the cash value, the policy will terminate if additional cash payments are not made.

Policyowners should consult with their tax advisors about the potential impact of any surrenders, withdrawals, or loans.

Endnotes

[i] Tax-Free Retirement. Patrick Kelly. April 2007.

[ii] Dominguez, Joe & Rubin, Vicki. Your Money or Your Life. Penguin Books, 1992.

[iii] http://www.quotesonfinance.com/quote/79/Albert-Einstein-Compound-interest

[iv] Weldon, Joel H. The Unlimited Times. Joel H. Weldon & Associates, Inc. 1997

[v] As told in a sermon by Pastor Gino Grunberg, Harbor Christian Center, Gig Harbor, Washington

[vi] This idea is credited to Larry Burkett

[vii] 2 Corinthians 9:6. The New International Bible

[viii] http://business.time.com/2012/08/21/the-six-daunting-financial-problems-facing-america. "The Six Daunting Financial Problems Facing America." Michael Sivy. August 21, 2012.

[ix] Social Security Administration. "About Social Security's Future …" Your Social Security Statement, pg. 1, col. 1&2, 2007.

[x] Social Security Administration. "The Future Financial Status of the Social Security Program." Social Security Bulletin, Vol. 70, No. 3, 2010. Stephen C. Goss

[xi] https://www.treasurydirect.gov/govt/reports/pd/histdebt/histdebt_histo5.htm

[xii] https://www.cbo.gov/publication/52298. "CBO's 2016 Long-Term Projections for Social Security: Additional Information." December 21, 2016

[xiii] truthinaccounting.org. July 26, 2017

[xiv] http://www.truthinaccounting.org/about/our_national_debt. July 26, 2017

[xv] usdebtclock.org. July 26, 2017

[xvi] Tax-Free Retirement. Patrick Kelly. April 2007.

[xvii] Internal Revenue Service, United States Department of the Treasury. IRS Publication 590 (2005). Individual Retirement Arrangements (IRAs). www.irs.gov/formspubs

[xviii] Forbes. "IRS Announces 2017 Tax Rates, Standard Deductions, Exemption Amounts And More." Kelly Phillips Erb. October 25, 2016.

[xix] As told in a sermon by Pastor Stuart Bond, Chapel Hill Presbyterian Church, Gig Harbor, Washington.

About the Author

Patrick Kelly is the author of seven books: Tax-Free Retirement (2007), The Retirement Miracle (2011), Stress-Free Retirement (2013), The 5 Retirement Myths (2015), Seven Secrets to a Happy Retirement (2016), The Life Insurance Dilemma (2017), and Tax-Free Retirement – 10th Anniversary Edition (2017). He resides in the Pacific Northwest with his wife of 27 years and their children. Patrick's "client first" philosophy is the centerpiece of all his messages.